THIS ISLAND NOW
THE B.B.C. REITH LECTURES 1962

By the same Author

*

THE TWICE BORN
A Study of a Community of High Caste Hindus

THIS ISLAND NOW

The B.B.C. Reith Lectures 1962

by

G. M. CARSTAIRS

Professor of Psychological Medicine
University of Edinburgh

1963
THE HOGARTH PRESS
LONDON

Published by
The Hogarth Press Ltd
42 William IV Street
London, WC2

*

Clarke, Irwin & Co. Ltd
Toronto

Printed in Great Britain by
T. & A. Constable Ltd
Hopetoun Street, Edinburgh

CONTENTS

Acknowledgements

During the writing of these lectures the author solicited and was generously given advice, help and suggestions by many individuals in addition to those whose works have been cited in the text. Among the first to be consulted was the Principal of Edinburgh University, Sir Edward Appleton (himself a former Reith Lecturer); others have included Professors Richard Titmuss, J. N. Morris and E. M. Gruenberg, Drs Neil Kessel, Henry Walton and Alwyn Smith, Mrs Margot Jeffreys and Miss Griselda Rowntree, Mr Percy Johnson-Marshall, Dr Leslie Wilkins and his colleagues in the Home Office Criminological Research Unit, the Rev. Campbell Maclean of Cramond Kirk and the Rev. James Blackie, Chaplain to the University of Edinburgh. Dr E. E. Krapf, Professor Robert Oppenheimer and Mrs Prudence Smith read preliminary drafts of certain lectures and contributed to their improvement. Invaluable research assistance was given by Mrs Mary Holland and also, at every stage, by the author's wife, Vera Carstairs. The producer, Miss Anna Kallin, applied her aesthetic and technical gifts, as well as an infinity of patience and encouragement, to helping the author to make his lectures approximate, at least in some degree, to the special requirements of the Spoken Word. The author is deeply grateful to the B.B.C. for the honour of being invited to deliver the 1962 Reith Lectures, and to all those who helped him so greatly in their preparation.

Acknowledgements are due also to the Editor of *The Scotsman* for permission to reproduce, in the Introduction, passages from an article on the Reith Lectures first published in *The Scotsman* on 24th December 1962.

Introduction

The Reith Lecturer is appointed each year by the invitation of the director-general of the British Broadcasting Corporation, after preliminary discussions with members of his staff. What goes on in these preliminary deliberations is the secret of the Corporation.

In former years, the debate may have turned merely upon whom to invite; but in 1962 the high councils of the B.B.C. went farther, and took the initiative in indicating, in very general terms, the theme to be covered. This was nothing less than a review of the State of the Nation, in the light of changes which have come about in the community and in private life since the beginning of the century.

Confronted with this formidable task, I must confess to having had profound misgivings. Only the realization that never in my life would I be offered such an opportunity again gave me the temerity to accept a commission which a wiser man would have—perhaps already had—declined.

From the start my intention was to scan the principal landmarks in our recent social history, to try to trace the changes which they have brought into our lives; and finally to speculate about the direction which our society is taking in the second half of the twentieth century.

To ascertain the facts and figures of recent social changes was not unduly difficult—the task was rather to pick out the most important elements from the voluminous documentation of our times. Social history is a firmly established discipline in British intellectual life; but the same cannot be said for sociology, and particularly not for that branch of sociology which investigates the interaction of environment and personality. Here, American sociologists have undoubtedly led the way.

In academic theses and in books designed for wider readership many U.S. social scientists (and not a few psycho-analysts) have tackled this theme.

I personally had come late to the study of social anthropology after having completed my training in medicine and psychiatry. In Britain I found that Culture and Personality studies were viewed, on the whole, with disfavour; but it was quite another matter when I spent a post-graduate year in the U.S.A. There I enjoyed the stimulus of meeting able anthropologists such as Kroeber, Herskovits, Linton, Cluckhohn, Hallowell and Leighton who had contributed to the theoretical structure of this class of studies. In 1949 I was privileged to attend the seminars conducted by Dr Margaret Mead and her co-workers in their Study of Culture at a Distance.

American social scientists have not only led the way in combining personality development theory with field observation; they have also been among the first to apply the techniques of social anthropology to sub-cultures and to particular social institutions (such as the mental hospital) in their own multi-faceted society.

If these lectures had been delivered in America, their main themes might well have been the same; the problems of child-rearing, of adolescence, and of the changing status of women are similar in Britain and in the U.S.A., as are the indicators of social malaise and personal maladaptation. The greatest difference might have been found in the reaction of the audience. My impression is that American readers are more accustomed than are the British to having their accepted values submitted to the dispassionate scrutiny of social research, and can tolerate such a process with equanimity. This remains to be seen. It was certainly not the case in the United Kingdom. For some weeks after the delivery of the third lecture the correspondence columns of the entire British press, from the national dailies and weeklies down to local parish magazines, seemed to reverberate with discussion of the alarming suggestion that sexual morality may, in fact, be changing before our eyes. The implication that before long premarital intercourse, with safeguards against conception, may become part of the experience of every maturing boy or girl raised a storm of protest, and a counter-demonstration from those who welcomed this eventuality.

It is difficult, in the social sciences, to keep value-judgments completely out of the picture: indeed I should say that it is impossible to do so, and consequently it is better that one's value-judgments be made explicit rather than left implicit. The latter was the case in the third lecture.

Since it appeared I have repeatedly been challenged to make my own position clear. I find myself in agreement with my critics on many points; we all would like sexual relationships to be accompanied by depth of feeling and by consideration for the welfare of one's partner; we all deplore casual promiscuity and its attendant risk of venereal disease; we all would like marital relationships to be stable and harmonious, for the sake of the parents' and even more of the children's happiness. Where we differ is that I believe that sexual experience before marriage may actually help towards achieving these goals.

There were, however, many other elements besides teenagers and sex in the six lectures. Two themes in particular kept recurring in different particular contexts: first, the sudden acceleration in the rate of social change, which tends to outstrip our conceptual grasp; and, second, the interplay of scientific observation and analysis on the one hand and the flights of creative imagination on the other.

The first theme found many illustrations, instances where events appeared to have outstripped most people's thinking. In my mind the most urgent instance of all is our failure to comprehend the full significance of the hydrogen bomb.

As I write, Mr Macmillan is engaged in negotiating for the

Polaris rocket to be the carrier of our nuclear weapons; and yet, as Lord Mountbatten reminded us quite recently, and as we all know at the back of our minds, these weapons spell destruction, not only to our enemies but to ourselves. Mankind itself is in a near-suicidal frame of mind; and if we do not soon awaken to a clear realization of the danger of this situation, Armageddon may literally be upon us.

The other theme, the counterpoint of intellectual understanding and creative imagination, was reflected in the choice of a line from W. H. Auden ('Look, Stranger at this Island Now') for the title of the series, and a phrase from T. S. Eliot's 'Murder in the Cathedral' for one sub-title ('Living and Partly Living'), and the recourse, in the final talk, to Hugh McDiarmid's eloquent line: 'Earth, thou bonnie, broukit bairn,' as an illustration of an art form rooted in a particular community's traditions. Here, however imperfectly expressed, was what I myself had learned as a result of the strenuous exercise of preparing these lectures: the importance of keeping intellectually abreast with events in a fast-changing world community, while still keeping imaginatively in touch with the creative artists, the poets or Makars, first of our own and then of other lands.

I

THIS ISLAND NOW

I

This Island Now

Looking back it now seems that our concept of ourselves as a nation and people reached a peak of naïve self-esteem in late Victorian times, a heady altitude from which we have been descending ever since. We are not alone in this: other European countries have experienced similar changes of outlook. This change has been accelerated by two world wars and by radical technological and political changes throughout the world; but a change of temper was apparent long before these developments. Formerly, our attitude to the rest of the world was outward-looking. We annexed, administered and developed large areas and sent missionaries to convert their peoples to our religion in the conviction that we were doing all this for their own good as well as ours. Then gradually this tide turned. We found it less easy to be quite sure that our way of life was necessarily the best.

It is, I believe, significant that it was at the very time when our imperial self-image began to fade and when fewer young people were coming forward as missionaries that there was a quickening of interest and research in social anthropology. The institutions and values of so-called 'primitive' societies became subjects of serious study as ways of life different, but not necessarily inferior, to our own. More recently these techniques of inquiry have been focussed upon aspects of our own society which had long been ignored or taken for granted.

There had, of course, been earlier examples of sociological research in Britain, studies of conditions of employment, of housing and of poverty which paved the way to social reforms.[1] These studies were inspired by a developing social conscience. They were concerned to show that the standards valued by an educated minority were unattainable by most members of our community. Such studies are still needed, and are still going on. But in the last few years we have seen the beginning of research of a different kind, in which our own institutions and values, and the means by which they are transmitted from generation to generation, are critically examined in the light of comparative studies in many other cultures. A great deal of the fascination of social anthropology has lain not merely in its enlargement of our knowledge of the range of established patterns of human behaviour but even more in its capacity to give us a better understanding of our own. No doubt the great change in Britain's political and economic position in the world has contributed towards our becoming a more inward-looking society, but social anthropology has provided the means by which this new attitude can find expression.

In these talks I am going to discuss some recent findings concerning that perennial pursuit: the study of man. This means the study of man in society because human behaviour can only be understood in its social context. As Professor Medawar showed in the last of his Reith Lectures,[2] the legacy of cultural traditions is part of each man's inheritance and contributes, along with the biological endowment of his genes and the circumstances of his upbringing, to the formation of his adult personality.

I shall concern myself particularly with the interaction of tradition, social environment and personality in our own changing society, and I shall choose for particular examination a number of areas in which things seem to have gone wrong—indicators of malaise in our community today. In so doing I shall display my own special concern, which is to use the study of society as a means to a better understanding of my fellow-men.

In Britain, anthropologists such as Rivers,[3] Seligman[4] and Malinowski[5] were among the first to direct attention to the impact of social pressures upon personality development, but for more than a generation now the main emphasis in British anthropology has been on the analysis of social structure. One has to remember that in the early days field work was usually carried out in distant isolated communities whose relatively fixed and stable institutions lent themselves to this type of analysis, although in his later years Malinowski[6] himself became increasingly preoccupied with studying the stresses and shifts which occur in societies undergoing rapid change.

In recent years anthropologists have carried out studies in local communities in Britain, communities which were only partly isolated and much involved in change.[7] The interest of these studies has been to show that one can still recognize distinctive local patterns of kinship ties, of shared experiences, attitudes and patterns of behaviour in these separate groups or sub-cultures of our society. Even in highly mobile societies such as ours some basic elements of kinship structure still persist.

Meanwhile in America a new subject for research has been developing through the collaboration of social anthropologists and psychologists with a common interest in personality development. This is the study of culture and personality and especially that branch of the study which has come to be called 'studies in national character'. The attribution of peculiar characteristics to members of alien communities is as old as history—certainly as old as Caesar or Herodotus. Neither Herodotus nor his successors were at all inhibited in making sweeping generalizations about the character of the peoples whom they described.

Over the years certain stereotypes about the characteristics of different peoples have been established by successions of travellers' tales. But it is only in the present century that this impressionistic account of the characteristics of other peoples has given place to more systematic study. It was necessary first of all to stop attributing human differences solely to genetic variations. Increasingly it has come to be recognized that the differences between peoples are not merely biological but are differences rather in the way they learn to behave.

The study of human personality and its development had to await, indeed is still awaiting, a systematic theory which would command general acceptance, a theory which would combine and do justice to the different elements in the process of developing the adult personality. It would take into account, first, the biological inheritance conveyed by the genes, which largely determines a man's physical characteristics (including his body chemistry) and his temperament; secondly, the material circumstances of his growing years with particular reference to nutrition and health; and, most important of all, his learning experiences. In every society, even before we are old enough to talk, we begin to be told things, told the names of things, told how to behave: in this way we learn what to expect of the natural world and of our fellow-men.

It was linguists, and particularly Benjamin Whorf,[8] writing in the late 'thirties and early 'forties, who pointed out that the very process of learning our native language determines to a large extent the way in which we perceive the world and our fellow-men, because each language embodies within its structure and vocabulary the transmission of ideas held by that particular community. Even familiar words, words like 'sister' or 'home' or 'future', convey various shades of meaning in different languages; and every language has some words—such as *dharm-bahin* in Hindustani—whose meaning cannot readily be translated into any other tongue except by an explanatory phrase.

Among anthropologists Benjamin Whorf's contemporary Ralph Linton[9] was especially clear-thinking in his analysis of the different ingredients, the deliberate and the tacit forms of learning, which contribute to the acquisition of adult roles in a differentiated society. He and Abram Kardiner[10] developed the useful concept of the 'basic personality type', the paradigm of the normal human being, which turns out to be different for each particular culture; but psychologists in general have not yet reached agreement about the processes involved in human learning.

There are at present two important and apparently conflicting explanations of the way in which we acquire our adult characteristics: one, which has come to be known as 'learning theory', contends that we learn as experimental animals do, in response to similar laws of drive, reward, repetition, punishment and extinction—and that is all. Advocates of this theory point to its economy of hypotheses, and to the way in which it lends itself to experimental verification. Its critics concede that it serves extremely well to systematize the processes of deliberate learning and teaching—it has already led to the invention of highly ingenious 'teaching machines'. In my opinion, however, a serious defect of learning theory is that it does not do justice to the emotional and irrational aspects of human personality; and yet these are too important to be overlooked.

The other school of thought is represented by the psychoanalysts, who do not speak with one voice but who at least show certain areas of agreement; they assert the profound influence upon our everyday behaviour of thoughts and feelings of which we are usually unconscious; and they stress the importance of events in the first five years of life in shaping those aspects of our adult personalities of which we tend to be least aware. We all know that human infants are endowed with strong feelings long before they are capable of speech, or of grasping rational concepts; psycho-analysts maintain that from early infancy we experience a vivid fantasy life which continues to influence us, in subterranean fashion, in our later years.

The real antithesis between these two points of view lies in the importance which psycho-analysts attribute to the instinctual side of mental life, most of which is unconscious but finds

expression in dreams and irrational fears, in fantasy and involuntary actions. It was Freud's revelation of the life-long influence of the unconscious mind upon our adult characteristics
which introduced a change in psychological understanding
comparable to the Copernican revolution in astronomy.

The great appeal of Freudian theory was that it gave promise
of providing a key which would enable us to decipher some of
the most bafflingly incomprehensible elements in human experience—above all, the apparently irrational features in
human motivation. It is in America that psycho-analysis has
received the fullest acceptance in the academic sphere as well as
in its clinical application; so it is not surprising that it is
American anthropologists who have been among the first to
employ psycho-analytic techniques in their field work on
culture and personality, and psycho-analytic theories in their
interpretation. This collaboration of disciplines was already
apparent in the early works of Margaret Mead, a brilliantly
intuitive psychologist who set herself the task of unravelling
the respective share of constitutional inheritance and social
learning in personality development in a series of field studies—
first, of the crisis of adolescence (or rather, its apparent absence)
in Samoan society, and then of child-rearing and adult roles in
six Melanesian cultures.[11] Later Dr Mead began to apply the
same techniques of observation and interpretation to studies of
contemporary American child-rearing and its end results. Her
studies, and those of her teacher, Ruth Benedict,[12] gave promise
of a great advance in the precision with which national characteristics could be described and their origins traced to crucial
formative experiences.

During the Second World War this minor division of
anthropology assumed a sudden importance: it became imperative to know, or at least to predict with fair accuracy,
what the Germans and the Japanese were like; and how they,
or the peoples temporarily under their control, would react to

important events in the course of the war. Several anthropologists (including the Britons Gregory Bateson and Geoffrey
Gorer) were employed on these studies, whose most important
achievement was the successful prediction, by Ruth Benedict
herself, of the way the Japanese people would react after their
Emperor's capitulation. This study was later published in her
book, *The Chrysanthemum and the Sword*.[13]

Since 1945, perhaps as a consequence of the struggle between
the U.S.A. and Russia for ascendancy in the world, America
has continued to be the principal, though no longer the only,
centre of research in national character. This research has been
far from disinterested: one notices, for example, that Columbia
University's seminars devoted to research in contemporary
cultures were subsidized by the Office of Naval Research[14]; and
a great deal of recent research into people's attitudes and values
has been undertaken by advertising agencies. But the fact that
these researches were undertaken for specific, and entirely non-
scientific reasons, does not necessarily affect their intrinsic
interest and value. A better understanding of the way members
of communities think and behave has many positive applications for education and community planning. It is of especial
interest in so far as it leads to a better understanding of social
pathology; and there is always the hope that it may help us to
clarify the processes which culminate in mental illness, or in
simple unhappiness and social inefficiency.

Perhaps I ought to make my own theoretical position clear.
As I see it, the dispute among these rival theories of personality
development has been taken to unnecessary extremes. Both
'sides'—which we may describe as the behaviourists on the one
hand and the psycho-analysts on the other—have done enough
valuable work to make possible a scientific attitude which is
indebted to both. One has first to learn to avoid the rigidity of
either extreme position. After all, those who believe that
humans are only a more complicated species of laboratory

animal, whose behaviour patterns and responses can in the end be exhaustively described, are really putting forward the psychological equivalent of Newtonian theory in physics; but, as Professor Oppenheimer told us in an earlier series of Reith Lectures,[15] even in physics the concepts of pure objectivity and of absolute determinism cease to be applicable in the study of ultimate single events, where precise statements are replaced by the expression of probabilities. In psychological research, too, probability theory plays an essential part because many of the variables can be measured only approximately; but diehard adherents of so-called learning theory believe that within these practical limitations they can provide the most accurate account available of how human personality is formed and the best predictions of how individuals or groups of individuals will react when exposed to specific experiences.

The psycho-analysts, on the other hand, believe that learning theory which is built upon objective experimental observations alone is doomed to give only an incomplete and sometimes misleading account of personality development because it leaves out one whole aspect of human experience on the grounds that it can be described only in subjective and unreliable terms. This is the area of the individual's inner life of emotion and fantasy, and especially the patterns of emotional expectations which are formed during early childhood. It seems to me undeniable that unconscious ingredients are indeed basic elements in the personality structure and do influence the individual's perceptions throughout his later life—including his perceptions of apparently impersonal situations such as a psychological test or a laboratory experiment. Long ago, D. H. Lawrence summed this up neatly, when he wrote: 'Anyone can say boo to a goose, but God alone knows what the goose hears.'[16]

But when some analysts go on to say that these inner processes of the emotional life can never be expressed in explicit and (however crudely at first) in quantitative terms but must be apprehended intuitively, then they are preaching a kind of mysticism which is inimical to a scientific approach and therefore to the growth and transmission of our knowledge. However eloquently they may describe their patient's deep motivations, these descriptions remain works of art, products of the analyst's creative imagination: they do not add to our knowledge of the processes involved. I think the reason for this—as I would call it—aberration is that in the early years of this century Freud and his followers had to contend with fiercely vituperative opposition. As a result, the analytic movement has at times tended to take on some of the emotional attributes of a persecuted religious sect rather than the self-critical qualities essential to scientific inquiry. But, need one say, some analysts are also scientists. They see no necessary antagonism between analytic theory and the requirements of scientific method; they would accept the need for analytic hypotheses to be formulated in terms which would enable them to be tested experimentally.

My own allegiance, then, is to the scientific approach in the study of personality development; an approach which will include, as a series of hypotheses worthy of further research and testing, the analytic account of our unconscious drives and our unconscious fantasies. This dispute is not purely academic. It is of vital importance for the understanding of neurosis and psychopathy, and it contributes to knowledge about more crippling mental disorders; but it also has an important bearing on educational theory, on how we should bring up our children —and on the diagnosis of some of the social ailments which are becoming increasingly conspicuous in our community. Once infectious disease was the principal cause of death and disability; but now it is from other sources that we encounter threats to life and to the fullness of living.

The science which underlies the practice of preventive medicine is epidemiology—the study of the distribution of disease.

Today this science is confronted with new challenges. It has to deal with ill-defined illnesses of gradual onset, such as cardio-vascular disease, psychosomatic disorders and the psycho-neuroses, that is, with crippling rather than with killing diseases, whose cause has to be sought not in the attacks of hostile organisms but rather in the individual himself and in his habits. His behaviour, his diet, his mode of life and his personal relationships all may play a part in their development. But which science can offer us the diagnosis, or suggest the remedy, for the signs of sickness in society itself? Here we are on less sure ground, where the social sciences themselves are only beginning to find their feet.

They will gain in assurance (and in wider acceptance) if they succeed in showing that they can offer first a precise delineation of the phenomena they deal with—such as marital disharmony, parental deprivation, delinquency, alcoholism, psychopathy, indeed all the indicators of social and personal disorganization. The next step is to construct a series of hypotheses about the processes underlying these phenomena, hypotheses which can be tested by experiment or by subsequent observations. It is in this less certain field of the diagnosis of the causes of social malaise that the techniques of social anthropology and of developmental psychology come to be employed; and it is here that I see scope for the development of important new appli-cations of the study of social learning.

As I hope to show, the skills used in studying 'national character' can be directed towards throwing light on areas of malaise in our own society. At first sight this seems strange, because all the early 'culture and personality' studies were carried out in small, homogeneous and stable societies. Our society is large and heterogeneous; but it contains within it a number of sub-cultures, each with a mode of life and a system of values which influence the behaviour of its members; and each is changing, just as many of the tribes described by the anthropologists are changing so rapidly that a contemporary analysis of their institutions soon becomes a document in their social history.

Not long ago I had an opportunity of revisiting the scenes of my own childhood which was spent in the mission compound of Nasirabad, a military cantonment in northern India. It was completely changed. The world I knew has vanished, although some of its monuments remain, adding to the litter of abandoned courts and disused temples which can be found all over India. That particular community of sahibs and memsahibs represented a special sub-culture of our society, if you like, and a relatively transitory one. Yet cannot the same be said of other sub-cultures in our society, groups drawn together by the shared circumstances of their lives? What has happened to the middle-class society of the 1920s—not the upper middle class whose sons went to Oxbridge as a matter of course and whose daughters' highest aspiration was to be presented at Court, but the middle middle class who went to church on Sundays, employed a cook and two housemaids, and embodied the solid bourgeois virtues? Their material culture has changed too. Their large houses have been subdivided into flats, the bell-pulls in their drawing-rooms pull no bells. They can no longer identify each other by their clothes or their accents; and their favourite holiday resorts have been invaded.

Other sub-groups were drawn together by shared deprivations rather than by privileges. Their common memories were of a narrow range of slum streets, of one or two crowded rooms, of squalor, hunger and insecurity. For many of these, too, the material circumstances of the 'twenties and 'thirties have radically changed. In each of these sub-groups a new amalgam is continually being formed, compounded of the memories of the older members, the experiences of today, and young people's hopes and fears for the future. In former times, human institutions remained unchanged through many

23

generations; then society's values seemed immutable and the individual had to be content to 'strut and fret his hour upon the stage', playing a part, but unable to alter the setting or the plot of the play. Now people are more aware that institutions are man-made, imperfect, requiring and capable of constant modification.

It may be that many of the social problems of our society today derive from this new personal awareness that the conditions of life can be altered and controlled, and from the accompanying impatience to see things change at once.

In medicine, pain and malaise have long been recognized as having a positive function, alerting the organism to threats to its well-being, if not to its survival, so that something will be done to meet the threat. I propose in my next lectures to examine in this light some of the indicators of pathology—of malaise in our society—in order to see whether the social sciences can suggest a diagnosis or can indicate what future developments these symptoms may presage.

NOTES

1 Booth, Charles. *Life and Labour of the People in London*. London, 1892–97.
  Rowntree, B. S. *Poverty, A Study of Town Life*. London, 1901 and 1922.
  Llewellyn Smith, H. *New Survey of London Life and Labour*. London: P. S. King, 1930.
  Webb, Beatrice. *My Apprenticeship*. London and New York: Longmans, 1926, latest re-issue 1950.
2 Medawar, P. B. *The Future of Man*. London: Methuen, 1960
3 Rivers, W. H. R. *Psychology and Ethnology*. London: Routledge & Kegan Paul. New York: Harcourt, Brace, 1926.
4 Seligman, C. G. 'Anthropology and Psychology', *J. R. anthrop. Inst.*, **54**, 13, 1924.

5 Malinowski, B. *Sex and Repression in Savage Society*. New York: Harcourt, Brace. London: Routledge & Kegan Paul, 1927. *The Sexual Life of Savages*, London: Routledge & Kegan Paul, 1929. New York: Halcyon House, 1929.

6 Malinowski, B. *The Dynamics of Culture Change*. New Haven, 1949.

7 Outstanding examples of these studies are:
Young, M. and Wilmott, *Family and Kinship in East London*. London: Routledge & Kegan Paul, 1957.
Williams, W. M. *The Sociology of an English Village, Gosforth*. London: Routledge & Kegan Paul, 1956.
Frankenberg, R. *Village on the Border*. Cohen & West, 1957.
Willmott, P. and Young, M. *Family and Class in a London Suburb*. London: Routledge & Kegan Paul, 1960.
Dennis, N., Henriques, F. and Slaughter, C. *Coal is our Life*. Eyre & Spottiswoode, 1956.

8 Whorf, B. 'The Relation of Habitual Thought and Behaviour to Language'. In Speir, Hallowell & Newman (Eds.), *Language, Culture and Personality*. Menasha, 1941. See also Carroll, J. B. (Ed.), *Language, Thought and Reality, Selected Writings of Benjamin Lee Whorf*. New York: Wiley & Sons, 1956.

9 Linton, R. *The Cultural Background of Personality*. New York: Appleton-Century. London: Routledge & Kegan Paul, 1945.

10 Kardiner, A. *The Individual and His Society*. New York: Columbia Univ. Press, 1939. *The Psychological Frontiers of Society*. New York: Columbia Univ. Press, 1945.

11 Mead, Margaret. *From the South Seas*. New York: Morrow, 1939.

12 Benedict, Ruth. *The Study of Cultural Patterns in European Nations*, Trans. N.Y. Acad. of Science Ser., II, 8, 274, 1946.

13 Benedict, Ruth. *The Chrysanthemum and the Sword*. Boston: Houghton Mifflin, 1946. London: Secker & Warburg, 1947.

14 Mead, Margaret and Metraux, Rhoda. *The Study of Culture at a Distance*. Univ. of Chicago Press, 1953 and Cambridge Univ. Press, 1953.

15 Oppenheimer, R. *Science and the Common Understanding*. London and New York: Oxford Univ. Press, 1954.

16 This observation occurs in his interesting and exasperating little book: Lawrence, D. H. *Fantasia of the Unconscious*. New York, 1922. London: Secker, 1923.

II

THE FIRST YEARS

II

The First Years

Many of the social changes which have occurred during this century must have influenced the physical and mental health, the moral values, the well-being of the people in this crowded island. I propose to begin at the beginning, by considering what has been happening to infants in their first years of life: and perhaps the most striking change is that babies born in the last two generations have had a much better chance of surviving into adult life[1]—so much so that our population has increased by more than one-third since this century began.[2] The historian, Peter Laslett, pointed the contrast with present-day experience recently by reminding us that a small coffin on the kitchen table was an all too familiar sight in working-class homes early in this century.[3] Among those who survived, many were stunted by chronic illness and under-nourishment. Nowadays when we talk of malnutrition we tend to think of the under-developed countries; yet as recently as 1937 more than half the inhabitants of these islands lived on a diet inadequate to maintain their health.[4] In my schooldays it was common to see children—and adults—crippled by the deficiency disease called rickets.

This type of cripple has almost disappeared from our midst; but there is another that is still with us, and in considerable numbers. I mean psychological cripples, people whose personalities have been warped at an early stage of their development, and who reveal this injury in the pattern of their adult lives. Do not think that I subscribe to the contemporary American habit of introducing psychiatric jargon into everyday life, so that instead of saying 'I can't stand that fellow', one assumes a superior expression and says 'He's a very sick man'. Our species is so agreeably diverse that it is bound to include many who find each other's personalities uncongenial. But have we not all known people who, even if they are clever and capable, are yet flawed by some persistent trait which prevents them from ever enjoying natural and easy relationships with their fellow-men? Sometimes these emotional cripples turn upon themselves, and are gnawed by dyspeptic pain or some other physical complaint; but all too often they make other people suffer as well, particularly their subordinates and their nearest kin. I do not know whether emotional cripples of this type are becoming commoner in our society; I think it is more likely that we are simply learning to recognize them more readily for what they are. When we do so, we become less exasperated by their behaviour, destructive though it is, and try to understand why their capacity for forming relationships with their fellows—perhaps the most important aspect of human personality—has remained so stunted and impoverished.

When does this mischief occur? To ask this is to raise the larger question: when do we acquire the characteristics of our adult personality? The Jesuits used to say that if you let them have a child for his first seven years he would never lose the stamp of their teaching; public schools make similar, if less sweeping, claims. Where does the process begin? Is it innate?

Certainly the potentiality for future personality development must be innate, and inherited factors probably influence the child's temperament as they do his physique; but modern research in ethology (which is the new name for the study of animal behaviour) has taught us to view instinct, even in animals, in a new light. It now appears that instinctive behaviour is seldom inherited entire and ready-made. Chaffinches, for example, have to learn from other chaffinches in order to develop their song to the full; if they are reared alone they achieve only a rudimentary chaffinch vocabulary, whereas if they are reared with larks they do their best to produce a different set of calls.[5] Similarly with other species: the ability to perform instinctive behaviour patterns is innate, but it is only fully developed through imitation and learning from others of their kind. Human beings surpass all other animals in their adaptability, in the large share which learning takes in their development: and this starts soon after their birth.

What happens to us in the first years of our life is of particular interest to psycho-analysts and cultural anthropologists. For the analyst, events and relationships experienced in infancy are believed powerfully to influence the structure of adult personality; for the anthropologist, childhood is the period in which we assimilate and build upon the inventions and discoveries of our forbears. As Margaret Mead has put it: 'A child who does not participate in this great body of tradition, whether because of defect, neglect, injury or disease never becomes fully human.'[6]

That is a striking concept, but a puzzling one: puzzling, because it implies the ability to recognize a point at which a child ceases to be deprived and becomes 'fully human'. This is not easy. In a highly differentiated society such as ours, children participate in tradition to a very different extent according to the amount of education which they receive; and this in turn is determined largely by the intelligence, interests and financial condition of their parents.

History and literature form so large a part of our traditions that one could almost say that only those who have had a sound education can become full participants in our society: but at the beginning of the century the great majority of our children could not hope to receive this amount of schooling, and thus the gulf between the educated and uneducated classes was widened. But it is not only a matter of education in the formal sense. Our early upbringing also influences the pattern of our feelings. This is why although a stranger can, with application, learn another people's language and customs very well indeed, yet full assimilation to that people will continue to elude him because he has been acquiring only the knowledge and skills which belong to later childhood and adolescence. He has not shared in the simple experiences of infancy which have already left their mark on that people's outlook and behaviour. To master the facts about a people and its folklore is easier than to share their feelings, because these have been acquired at a much earlier, pre-conscious stage of learning. This holds not only for the remote tribes which anthropologists study, but also for the several 'sub-cultures' which constitute a complex society like our own. The barrier between the middle class and the working class is not simply the result of differences in education; the barrier is due to an inability to share certain feelings rather than to a failure to understand what the other is saying.

Various experiences may be detrimental to this earliest learning; the gravest disruption of all occurs when an infant's relationship with its mother is broken by her absence, or her death. In recent years, the eloquent if sometimes controversial arguments of an English research worker, John Bowlby, have suggested the possibility that a child experiencing maternal deprivation in infancy may become peculiarly susceptible to psychiatric disorders in later life.[7] In some cases this leads to the development of the so-called 'affectionless character', an extreme example of the type of psychological cripple to whom I have already referred. Later studies, by Hilda Lewis[8] and by Bowlby's own group of research workers,[9] have tended to modify the supposition that separation invariably results in lasting damage to the child's personality, but they have confirmed that this happens in a considerable number of cases. In recent years Bowlby's argument has received fresh support from statistical studies carried out in Britain and America,[10] which have shown that among patients admitted to mental hospital the incidence of loss of a parent before the age of five is significantly higher than in others of like age in the general population; the difference was most marked for the early loss of the mother.

It is only now that we have learned how serious and how long-delayed the consequences of such a loss may be. This complete disruption of mother-child relationships by death or serious illness is much less common now than it was fifty or even thirty years ago; but what of the quality of that relationship when it is not interrupted? Bowlby claims that maternal deprivation occurs when mother and child fail to establish a 'warm, intimate and continuous relationship in which both find satisfaction and enjoyment'.[11]

It is difficult to believe that maternal care of this quality was very common in the slums of our large cities either in the early years of the century or during the depression of the nineteen-thirties—or even today. Close family ties can exist in spite of overcrowding and poverty—in the Gorbals of Glasgow they used to say 'the clartier the cosier'—but on the whole the younger children of a large slum family are unlikely to enjoy relationships with their harassed mothers 'in which both find satisfaction and enjoyment'. One suspects that this standard may prove too high to serve as the norm even for more privileged sections of the community. Many autobiographies of upper-class men and women—that of the Duke of Windsor is only one example—describe how severe maternal deprivation can occur when custom or the weight of other duties keeps a mother at a distance from her child.

The real challenge, to which a good deal of research is now being directed, is to identify the crucial events of the first two or three years of life, when that almost inseparable unit, the mother and her baby, interact to form the nucleus of a new personality. Analysis of this process directs attention to topics which prudishness formerly excluded from discussion—to things such as the small child's sexual feelings, his lively interest in his own excretory functions, the fear and hatred which he

33

THIS ISLAND NOW

sometimes feels towards one or other parent. All this may seem
at first both distasteful and curiously limited; but this is the
stuff of infancy. In the study of human personality we have to
reconcile ourselves to the fact that crude physical experiences
contribute to our psychic as well as to our bodily development.
Evolutionary biologists have taught us to regard ourselves as
mammals with an upright posture and with unusually dextrous
fore-paws, differing from most mammals in that we have no
breeding season and in that our offspring are born peculiarly
ill-equipped to fend for themselves. Human babies have to be
protected during an exceptionally long period of dependence,
and it is precisely during this prolonged state of helplessness
that the characteristically human attributes of learning and
imagination are developed. It is during these first years that, in
response to the promptings—for the most part implicit and
involuntary—of those persons who loom largest in his immediate surroundings the baby learns certain first lessons in how to
handle his feelings. This is indeed the crucial fact: that whereas
so many other aspects of our personality take years to develop,
we are born with the capacity to experience feelings—feelings
of pain, hunger, discomfort, to which babies give such whole-
hearted expression, and feelings of well-being and satiation
which, in the newborn, tend to induce sleep.

Coping with painful feelings is, then, the first task of psychological development, just as on the physical side coping with
hunger, thirst and cold is the first imperative need if we are to
survive. It is not too much to say that the way a mother handles
her child and his feelings will significantly influence that child's
future perceptions of the world and of his fellow-men. This
seems a bold statement, for which one is entitled to demand
supporting evidence. Psycho-analysts claim that their published
case material substantiates it; but to the critical reader, their
work usually lacks the elements necessary for a rigorous test
of their working hypotheses—their findings are plausibly

explained in terms of their theory, but the validity of the hypotheses themselves is not unequivocally demonstrated.

There have, however, been some confirmatory studies. For example, some years ago a psychologist, Dr Goldman Eisler,[12] carried out an experiment to test the Freudian theory that babies who are generously indulged at their mother's breast will acquire an habitual attitude of hopeful expectancy; whereas those who are less fortunate at this stage will grow up with a tendency to feel insecure and doubtful in their personal relationships. Her experiment verified this hypothesis: adults who in their infancy had been weaned early showed a significant bias towards a pessimistic outlook on the world, as compared with those who had been weaned late. In this century, we have seen several changes in what has been advocated as the best way to bring up babies. For a number of years paediatricians seemed preoccupied with schedules and formulae; now they have rediscovered the fact that suckling is an emotional experience for the child and not merely a taking-in of food.

Shortly after the Second World War, a survey was carried out of all babies born in England and Wales during one particular week—some 14,000 in all. At only eight weeks after their birth nearly half of these babies were found already to be exclusively bottle-fed.[13] What consequences result from this first experience? In the light of Dr Goldman Eisler's findings we could expect these children to grow up with a definite bias towards pessimism—and this indeed is the impression which we tend to give to visitors from other more exuberant societies.

Another basic experience in infancy is toilet training. Different societies, and different communities within our own society, vary widely in the degree of concern which attends this aspect of baby care. Some societies, including our own, seem to place an exaggerated emphasis upon the baby's being clean and dry as soon as possible. I say exaggerated emphasis, because most infants are not physiologically capable of this degree of control until they are well over a year old. If the mother fusses over it, the whole business of 'being clean' assumes an undue importance. Where this has happened, the child may grow up to be cautious, meticulous, over-conscientious, strict with himself and with those under his authority, perhaps parsimonious; in extreme degree, this can result in an obsessive-compulsive neurosis.

A majority of mothers in Britain still believe that toilet training should begin in the first months and should be completed within the first year.[14] They are doomed to disappointment, of course. In practice they find themselves fighting a losing battle with so-called 'naughty' children who are unable to conform to their expectations. An interesting corollary to this is the finding that in Britain there appears to be little belief in the inherent goodness of children.[15] Instead, parents attribute all sorts of malign and unruly tendencies to their growing infants; and they are prompted to do this, I believe, by their own unconscious conflicts. Their own early surrender to discipline has left unsatisfied a good many unruly impulses which find indirect expression in this anticipation of rebelliousness in their own children. It has other disadvantages also. We in Britain often congratulate ourselves on our patience and self-control—as exemplified in the orderly queues which we are so accustomed to join—but this docility may be won at the cost of surrendering a good deal of spontaneity and drive.

These basic features of child-rearing can be observed in any society, and have been incorporated in many culture-and-personality studies, including my own. When I lived for over two years in villages in the Aravli hills, in India, I became familiar with patterns of child care quite different from our own. Indian parents show none of our anxious concern for babies to be clean and dry as early as possible: that part of a child's training is attended to without fuss, and allowed to take its time. According to Freudian theory, this should be associated with an easy-going disregard for punctuality or precision over matters of detail, and that is what I found. My Hindu friends were aware of this difference between their ways and mine; at times they reproached themselves for their unreliability, at other times they teased me for my typically British habit of living by the clock.

Hindu babies have always enjoyed demand feeding. They are seldom far from their mother's side, and whenever they begin to fret their mother nurses them. It was only after my return to a block of flats in London that I realized how infrequently one hears a baby crying in India, how frequently in Britain.

I have already suggested that the early weaning of our babies may be responsible for the slight bias towards pessimism which colours our outlook. Among the Hindus whose personalities I studied, the opposite bias prevailed; they seemed to live in constant expectation of a stroke of good fortune. Each new acquaintance was scanned hopefully as if he might be the agent of their material and spiritual salvation; and in spite of many disappointments, these hopes would rise again.

In primitive societies, patterns of child rearing are slow to change. Each aspect of tribal custom is regarded as the only proper way to behave; often the wrath of the gods is believed to be incurred if traditional habits are broken. To some extent, the same is true of child-rearing in our own society. This has always been the domain of mothers and grandmothers, who have tended to cling to old familiar ways because until recent years they had relatively little education or experience of the wider world—certainly less than their daughters of the war and post-war years. It is, I believe, because of this time-lag in the modification of child-rearing practices that our emotional attitudes are sometimes anachronistic and ill-adapted to the changing realities of our society.

There undoubtedly exists a great discrepancy between what the developmental psychologist defines as optimal human relationships and the actual experience of most children in this country today. Granted that this is the case, is it of any significance? Does it have a bearing, for example, on the incidence of mental illness which, together with cancer and cardiovascular disease, presents one of the important unsolved problems of medicine today? Patients with mental disorders occupy nearly half the hospital beds of the National Health Service, but there are many more who experience minor nervous or emotional illnesses—in fact, at least one in every ten patients who consult their general practitioner is suffering from psychological rather than physical distress.[16]

I believe that in the major forms of mental breakdown, such as schizophrenia and manic-depressive psychosis, our most important advances in knowledge are likely to come not from psychological but from biochemical research; social and psychological factors can certainly contribute to the onset of these diseases and to their course, but their influence is probably secondary to crucial biological factors. The reverse is the case in the neuroses and psychosomatic disorders, which are so common as to enter into everyone's experience; here social and interpersonal factors are of primary importance. These illnesses are precipitated by stresses encountered by the adult patient, but as I have said their origin is often found in attributes of his own personality, which in turn is largely moulded by experiences of his earliest years.

The suffering of a neurotic patient may take forms which conceal its emotional origin. Often he complains of pain and physical exhaustion rather than of psychological symptoms such as anxiety or depression; but invariably one finds that these complaints occur in particular social contexts: certain quite ordinary experiences have a special meaning for him. The immediate stress is aggravated because it re-activates

38

painful experiences which occurred during those first years of emotional dependency.

I should like to emphasize that there is no such thing as a completely untraumatic upbringing—and this is not only because parents are fallible, but also because the infant's desires are sometimes so imperious that they must be disappointed. For all of us, frustrations alternate with gratifications, and in this our experiences differ from those of the neurotic only in degree. In a personal psycho-analysis, one comes to recognize neurotic traits in oneself; even without a personal analysis it is not difficult to recognize them in others.

A modicum of neurosis, then, is part of the normal human personality; it can even provide the stimuli for creative activity; it is only an excess which brings distress and incapacity. I believe that our present-day society has produced, and is still producing, a mass of avoidable neurotic suffering. This happens not deliberately, but out of ignorance—just as, until quite recently, unnecessary hardship was imposed on sick children by insisting on separating them from their mothers. It is impossible to legislate for love and affection; but at least we can help parents to recognize their children's emotional as well as their physical needs.

I have said that the origin of adult neurosis can be traced to the events of infancy. Paradoxically, this is not always true for the emotional disturbances of adolescence, which can often be better understood in terms of their current relationships. This is another way of saying that teenagers can be rebellious without being neurotically disturbed. Whereas an adult neurotic suffers because he is re-living painful relationships in his early life, for the adolescent and his parents the battle is still raging, and may be newly joined.

Earlier, I mentioned the traditions which still largely govern the way mothers handle their babies, and which are slow to change. In the world of adolescents, however, and in their relationships with their parents, changes have been dramatic. I believe this adolescent world deserves attention not only as a source of trouble, of public concern; but also because adolescents are themselves among the most active, as they are the most vociferous, agents of social change.

NOTES

1 The expectation of life at birth in 1901-10 was 45·8 for males and 52·4 for females, compared with 68·1 for males and 73·9 for females in 1958-60. At 5 years of age the expectation of life was: 55·9 for males and 58·5 for females 1901-10, 67·0 for males and 73·4 for females 1958-60. Registrar General's *Decennial Supplement to the Statistical Review of England and Wales 1921*, Part III. Registrar General's *Quarterly Statistical Return of England and Wales*, June 1961, No. 450, Appendix B. In the latter years of the last century the infant death-rate in Bethnal Green was twice as high as in St George's, Hanover Square. Registrar General's *Report for 1884* quoted in *Facts for Socialists*, Fabian Tract No. 5, 1908.

These figures show not only the great increase in expectation of life, but also the dramatic reduction in infant and child mortality rates. Infant mortality rates fall from 138 per 1,000 live births in 1901-05 to 66 per 1,000 live births in 1931 and 21 per 1,000 in 1961. Registrar General's *Statistical Review of England and Wales for 1960*, Part I, Table 3 (H.M.S.O. 1961) and *Report of the Ministry of Health for the Year 1961*, Part II (H.M.S.O. 1962).

2 The population of the U.K. rose from 38·2 millions in 1901 to 52·8 millions in 1961. This increase owed as much perhaps to the high birth-rate of late Victorian and Edwardian times as to the reduced mortality of this century.

3 Laslett, P. 'Social Change in England 1901-1951', *The Listener*, 28th Dec., 1961.

4 The extent of malnutrition in Britain in the 1930s was clearly indicated in Lord Boyd Orr's *Food, Health and Income*, London:

MacMillan, 1937⅞(2nd Edition), and in McGonigle and Kirby, *Poverty and Public Health*, London: Gollancz, 1936.

5 Thorpe, W. H. *Bird Song*, No. 12 of the Cambridge Monographs in Experimental Biology. Cambridge Univ. Press, 1961.

6 Mead, Margaret and Wolfenstein, M. (Eds.). *Childhood in Contemporary Cultures*. Chicago Univ. Press, 1955, p. 7.

7 Bowlby, J. *Maternal Care and Mental Health*. Geneva: W.H.O., 2nd ed. 1952.

8 Lewis, Hilda, *Deprived Children*. London: Oxford Univ. Press, 1954.

9 Bowlby, J., Ainsworth, Mary, Boston, M. and Rosenbluth, D. 'The Effects of Mother-Child Separation: a Follow-up Study', *Brit. J. med. Psychol.*, **29**, 211, 1956.

10 Quoted by Bowlby, J., in 'Childhood Mourning and the Implications for Psychiatry', *Amer. J. Psychiat.*, **118**, 481.
See particularly:
Hilgard, J. R. and Newman, M. F. *Psychiatry*, **22**, 113, 1909.
Hilgard, J. R., Newman, M. F. and Fisk, F.: *Amer. J. Orthopsychiat.*, **30**, 788, 1960.
Brown, F. 'Depression and Childhood Bereavement', *J. ment. Sci.*, **107**, 1961.

11 Bowlby, J. *Maternal Care and Mental Health*. Geneva, W.H.O., 2nd ed. 1952, p. 11.

12 Goldman Eisler, Frieda. Chapter in: *Personality in Nature, Society and Culture*. Eds. Kluckhohn, C. and Murray H. A. London: Cape. New York: Knopf, 2nd ed. 1953. This study was first reported in: *The Journal of Personality*, Vol. 17, pp. 83-103, 1948; Vol. 19, pp. 189-96, 1950; and the *Journal of Mental Science*, Vol. XCVII, pp. 765-82, 1951.
Dr Goldman Eisler makes it plain that while prolonged breast-feeding is significantly associated with the character trait of optimism, there is room for many other factors to contribute to the formation of this trait. Among those who have adduced evidence to show that experiences in early infancy are not

invariably or simply related to later personality development are:

Orlansky, H. 'Infant Care and Personality', *Psychol. Bull.*, Jan. 1949, and *Psychol. Rev.*, **46**, 1.

O'Connor, N., *Acta psychol.*, **12**, 174, 1956.

Wootton, Lady. *Social Science and Social Pathology* (Chapter V). London: Allen & Unwin, 1959.

13 Douglas, J. W. B. *Maternity in Great Britain.* London, Oxford Univ. Press, 1948.

14 Gorer, G. *Exploring English Character.* London: Cresset Press, 1955, p. 165.

15 Gorer, G. *Ibid.*, pp. 163, 178.

16 Kessel, W. I. N. 'Psychiatric Morbidity in a London General Practice', *Brit. J. prev. soc. Med.*, 1960, **14**, 16.

Shepherd, M., Fisher, M., Stein, L. and Kessel, W. I. N., *Proc. R. Soc. Med.*, 1959, **52**, 269.

III

VICISSITUDES OF ADOLESCENCE

III

Vicissitudes of Adolescence

I am going to talk about teenagers and that means, almost inevitably, that I am going to talk about violence and sex; but I should like to make it clear from the start that I regard the present increase of crimes of violence and the present state of confusion in the rules governing sexual behaviour as problems not only of adolescence but of our society as a whole. I believe that juvenile delinquency and sexual promiscuity can be regarded as pointers to areas of uncertainty, of confused values, in contemporary adult life.

Adolescence is, after all, the period of apprenticeship to one's adult role. There can be no doubt that this apprenticeship is *not* working smoothly just now. If we begin by considering crime and violence, we are confronted by some astonishing facts. There are nearly three times as many men in our prisons today as there were in 1938,[1] and nearly half of all the indictable offences are committed by youths under the age of twenty-one.[2]

This increase in crime was the more remarkable because it reversed a long-standing trend. Early in this century crime (and especially theft) was associated with poverty, and it was believed that when extremes of poverty were relieved, crime would diminish. Up to a point, this did in fact occur. Two exhaustive surveys of London Life and Labour, published at the turn of the century and in 1930 showed that during that period the incidence of severe penury had been greatly reduced —and that the crime rate had also diminished.[3]

Today, few schoolchildren are compelled to work; the majority receive pocket-money on a scale which would (and often does) startle their grandparents. As soon as they leave school, boys and girls can earn wages which enable them to spend so freely that whole industries exist to cater for their tastes. Whatever makes our adolescents rebellious and unruly, it is not penury.

Adolescents differ from us who have grown older in the strength of their feelings, and in their longing for certainties; they want to believe in something and they lapse into cynicism only when there seems to be nothing to believe in. They are capable of acting generously and disinterestedly: for example, I regard the teenagers' readiness to march in support of nuclear disarmament as an indication of their social responsibility.

The so-called 'adolescent crisis' has been a favourite subject for study by psychologists, sociologists and anthropologists. It was, indeed, the theme of Margaret Mead's first field work, in 1926, when she lived for nine months in village communities in Samoa.[4] She set herself the questions: 'Are the disturbances which vex our adolescents due to the nature of adolescence itself or to the civilization? Under different conditions does adolescence present a different picture?' She discovered that in Samoa adolescent stress and turmoil was as exceptional as it is usual in Western society, and she attributed this ease of transition to certain characteristics of Samoan society—its prevailing casualness, the absence of deep interpersonal relationships either within the family or between friends; and, as in most simple, homogeneous cultures, the absence of choice in matters of belief and conduct.

There was, she believed, much less neurosis among Samoans than among Americans, and she ascribed this to differences in their early experiences—particularly to the diffusion of personal relationships among many kinsfolk instead of their intensification in small self-contained family units, and to the tolerant acceptance of sexual experience as one of the pleasurable facts of life.

Another element in Samoans' upbringing which may have protected them against neurosis was their familiarity, as children, with the biological realities. Not only sex, but birth and death were frequent events in Samoan households, and they were not concealed; children learned about death and corruption, about birth and labour pains as a matter of course—learned to accept them as the penalties of being alive—just as sexual dalliance was among the rewards. In contrast, Western children are increasingly sheltered from contact with any of these events, which tend as a result to become mysterious and emotionally disturbing.

In Samoa, there was a stable society offering a strictly limited choice of adult roles. There have been times, long ago, when our society showed a similar continuity: but the opposite has been the case during the present century, in which the social environment of each generation is radically different from that of its predecessor.

I have repeatedly referred to the changes in our people's health and nutrition; but changes have been no less marked in popular education and types of employment. Nowadays we take universal basic education so much for granted that we forget how recent an acquisition it is; yet only in this century have more than half of the parents in our population had an efficient elementary education. In some respects we are not so far, after all, from countries like India, whose literature was until recently accessible only to a privileged minority.

Throughout the century, great changes have taken place in industrial techniques, and perhaps the greatest change is coming about now, with the spread of automation. These changes have had important repercussions upon family life, upon children's upbringing and perhaps especially upon their attitudes to authority. Traditionally, one of the functions of the family has been to reconcile children to the restraints on their behaviour which society expects them to obey. In a patriarchal society, such as ours has been—though this is changing—it is supposed to be the father who imposes these restraints.

47

Every child has to submit to a great deal of frustration of immediate desires and impulses in the process of growing-up. This frustration can be more readily tolerated if it is imposed by parents on whose support and affection the child knows he can rely; and socially acceptable patterns of behaviour can best be learned by the child's taking such parents as the models for his own adult role.[5]

At one time it was assumed that filial and parental feelings were natural and would develop spontaneously. In fact, however, in their complexity they are a typical example of human behaviour which has to be learned. A child's feelings towards his or her parents often include violent alternations between affection, anger and rivalry. The ability to establish a lasting truce in these feelings depends on how well they get on together, while the child grows towards maturity.

But you may well ask how I define that elusive concept, maturity. I suggest that the mature person shows these attributes: a realistic grasp of his environment, a sense of conviction about his own identity, an ability to cope with his practical tasks and an ability to establish deep mutual relationships with other people. None of these, obviously, are inborn attributes; they all have to be learned, and they are learned in stages. As the child grows he masters successive stages of physical accomplishment, of intellectual understanding and of mastery of anxiety; after each step forward there is a pause for consolidation. At adolescence comes the real challenge: is one ready to relinquish parental support, to be independent? At this time all the anxieties which were aroused at the earlier stages tend to be re-animated, and most prominent now is what Erikson has called the crisis of identity,[6] the pressing question: 'Who am I?' In their attempt to answer this question, adolescents frequently try out various roles, identify themselves with gangs or indulge in hero-worship. In earlier times the resolution of this problem was easier because they were confronted with only a few traditional occupations from which to choose, but now the range of choice is bewildering. Still, however, the young person's relationship with the parent of the same sex is of crucial importance.

If all goes well, a boy identifies himself with his father and accepts him as an ally; but if the father fails him (and this is more likely to happen at a time when the father's own self-confidence is precarious) then this truce is not declared, the boy's conflict of feelings remains unresolved, he finds himself a prey to sudden accesses of uncontrollable anger and destructive-ness which seem quite wanton and senseless to the outside observer—as indeed they are to the boy, who so often lamely and yet truthfully pleads that he 'doesn't know what made him do it'.

Children who have not had this guidance are less likely to fit into society; successive studies have shown that delinquency is commonest in families where the father has been missing because of death or desertion or absence on war service during his son's early years.[7] But fathers can also abdicate their role. This happened to some extent during the great depression of the 1930s (which was followed by a minor wave of delinquency when the small boys of that period reached late adolescence) and it appears to be happening again now. In reply to a recent questionnaire about the bringing up of children, a surprising number of working-class fathers expressed the view that children should be taught discipline 'by the State'.[8]

If we turn to consider young people's sexual behaviour today, we encounter many vehement opinions, but little reli-able information. There has been no Kinsey survey in Britain. It is frequently asserted that teenagers today are precociously active in sex relationships. On purely biological grounds, this need not surprise us because one of the consequences of im-proved health and nutrition has been a steady lowering of the age of puberty: a hundred years ago the mean age at which girls began to menstruate was 17 years, now it is $13\frac{1}{2}$.[9] In keeping with this physiological change, the mean age of marriage had declined during the present century[10]; but there is still a delay of several years between the time when young people are physically ready for sexual experience and their becoming either emotionally mature or economically independent. Precisely at this time modern advertising, films and popular reading expose them to constant sexual stimulation.

The increasing number of cases of venereal disease in young people, and the fact that in 1961 no less than 31 per cent. of girls who married while in their teens were pregnant at the time of their wedding,[11] are two indications of precocious sexual behaviour in our society. And yet, what do we mean by 'precocious'? Biologically children are capable of enjoying sexual relationships from the age of puberty. In many societies they are positively encouraged to do so; every Trobriand Island boy and girl, every young Samoan, every young member of Indian jungle tribes like the Maria has had many sexual experiences before their betrothal and wedding. The interesting thing is that this pre-marital licence has been found to be quite compatible with stable married life. I believe that we may be quite mistaken in our alarm—at times mounting almost to panic—over young people's sexual experimentation. Contraception is still regarded as something wicked, threatening to chastity, opening the way to unbridled licence. But *is* chastity the supreme moral virtue? In our religious traditions the essence of morality has sometimes appeared to consist of sexual restraint. But this was not emphasized in Christ's own teaching. For Him, the cardinal virtue was *charity*, that is consideration of and concern for other people. It was His intemperate disciple, Paul, an authoritarian character, who introduced the concept of celibacy as an essential part of Christian teaching.[12] And centuries later it was the reformed libertine, St Augustine, who placed such exaggerated emphasis upon the sinfulness of sex. It has always been those whose own sexual impulses have been precariously repressed who have raised the loudest cries of alarm over other people's immorality. As I have said, many societies get on quite well without pre-marital chastity. It seems to me that our young people are rapidly turning our own society into one in which sexual experience, with precautions against conception, is becoming accepted as a sensible pre- liminary to marriage; a preliminary which makes it more likely that marriage, when it comes, will be a mutually con- siderate and mutually satisfying partnership.

I have been talking so far as though our society were a single cultural unit, with consistent attitudes to such things as violence and sex; but this is far from being the case. At the end of last century, the gulf between the lives of different classes was so wide that when sociologists like Charles Booth[13] or Beatrice Webb[14] lived among working-class people their first-hand descriptions were as full of novel discoveries as an anthro- pologist's first reports about a primitive culture. Our literature and our history-books have been so permeated with the con- cerns of the educated classes that it is easy to forget that they have always been a privileged minority group. When Dickens, or in our century Jack London,[15] described the life of the London poor, they seemed to their readers to be writing about a different people, leading a different life. It was the same else- where in Europe: in Vienna, for example, the young Sigmund Freud was struck by the contrast between his own relatively sheltered middle-class upbringing and the hardships of the common people. He noted the contrast between typical middle-class restraint and working-class abandon, and specu- lated whether these traits might be influenced by the assurance of material comfort on the one hand and the constant threat of penury on the other. He ends a letter to his future wife with the words: 'I will not follow these thoughts further, but one might show how the common people judges, believes, hopes and works quite otherwise than we do. There is a psychology of the common man which is somewhat different from ours. . . .'[16]

Unfortunately he never did follow these particular thoughts further; if other interests had not claimed him, he might have become a pioneer of social psychiatry. Had he seriously pursued this line of thought he would presumably have tried to unravel the early emotional experiences of patients from poor homes as well as those of his bourgeois clientele, and by so doing he might have added another dimension to his theory of personality formation.

Perhaps it is easier to recognize contrasts like this in alien cultures. That, at least, was my experience during my anthropological field-work in India. I became aware of the very striking differences in attitudes to sex and violence in two of the communities which I studied, the high-caste Hindus who lived in settled villages, and the Bhils, a warlike tribe who inhabited the nearby jungles. High-caste Hindus enjoin a very strict taboo on any public display of sexual interest or even of affection; they teach their children to cultivate control over their emotions; it is not seemly to laugh out loud, to give open expression to feelings of any kind—but especially unseemly to give way to anger. By contrast, the Bhils delight in ardent love affairs, which they celebrate in song, and they are familiar with aggression; older Bhil children sometimes even strike their parents—which would be almost unthinkable in Hindu society. Their aggressive feelings are not overwhelming, nor alarming, but are harnessed to their preferred activities of hunting, abducting cattle or girls from other Bhil villages, and pursuing the feuds which follow a successful raid. The Bhils have succeeded in turning their aggressive energies to constructive use—constructive at least in terms of their boisterous way of life.[17]

Months later, when I came to analyse my field notes, I realized that this antithesis between Hindus and Bhils mirrored, in exaggerated form, the difference between middle-class and working-class attitudes to sex and to aggression in our own society.

Life in working-class streets is tougher than that in middle-class suburbs. In the former, disputes are more open and more often lead to blows. This is true, too, for expressions of sorrow and gaiety, as well as for anger. In contrast, emotional reserve is cultivated by the middle class and by those who aspire to middle-class status. Their feelings tend to be bottled up and their anger smoulders underground or is turned against themselves. A good deal of nagging ill-health may be caused by feelings, especially hostile feelings, which persist but are disavowed and denied expression.

If a Kinsey Survey were to be carried out in Britain we could expect findings different from his in America, reflecting our community's different attitudes towards sex. But I think it most likely that one of his findings would be confirmed: that is that young people from middle-class and from working-class backgrounds—defined by Kinsey as those who have college educations and those who have not—deal with their sexual urges differently. Middle-class youths try to practise prolonged sexual restraint; they masturbate and feel guilty about it. Young people of the working-class tend to have sexual experience more often from an earlier age.

Teenage sex and teenage violence are predominantly problems of the urban working class and they serve as a reminder of the continuing stress between the privileged and the under-privileged in our society. I believe that the chief reason for the persistence of social class division is the continuing inequality of educational opportunity in our country. It is true that we have taken a great step forward in the years just after the Second World War, but we still lag behind America in this respect and far behind the U.S.S.R. An enormous amount of ability still remains undeveloped. In Britain today 75 per cent.

of children finish their full-time education at the age of 15.[18]

Teenagers find it difficult to resist the immediate rewards of relatively well-paid unskilled work; but having once entered such jobs they come to realize, after a year or two, that they will never be able to earn substantially more.

There is more social mobility in Britain today than ever before, but it is still limited, and still stressful for those who do break through. At the same time the popular press, radio, television and films perpetually flatter their audiences by assuming that they are familiar with a level of material comfort and sophistication which seldom corresponds to their actual experience. The real advances in standards of living have been outstripped by this constant stimulation of material aspirations.

Much of the delinquency shown by working-class youth can be viewed as protest behaviour, a protest not so much against their present hardships as expressing their feeling that there are a lot more good things in life which they would like to have but which are still beyond their reach. It is a gesture of defiance against a society which appears to ignore their predicament, a gesture which is more likely to be made when relationships with their parents are faulty. In fact, all too often such youths lack support where they need it most. Edward Blishen, a singularly compassionate schoolteacher, has described a sub-culture of our society, that of the urban secondary modern school, where one child in three seemed never to have received the assurance of parental affection.[19]

This poverty of human relationships can be found elsewhere, but it seems most frequent in city slums; It is perhaps the legacy of a squalid century of substandard living. In the more distant past, even if parental affection was lacking, working-class children grew up in a community which had strong views of right and wrong; this morality perhaps owed more to the solidarity of a group which had shared rough times than to the formal Christian ethics in which better-class children were instructed. Today, however, both the popular and the church-going types of morality have slipped into disuse. Popular morality is now a wasteland, littered with the debris of broken convictions. Concepts such as honour, or even honesty, have an old-fashioned sound; but nothing has taken their place. The confusion is perhaps greatest over sexual morality; here the former theological canons of behaviour are seldom taken seriously. In their place a new concept is emerging, of sexual relationships as a source of pleasure, but also as a mutual encountering of personalities in which each explores the other and at the same time discovers new depths in himself or herself. This concept of sex as a rewarding relationship is after all not so remote from the experience of our maligned teenagers as it is from that of many of their parents. It bears no resemblance at all to the unromantic compromise between sensuality and drudgery which has been the lot of so many British husbands and wives in the past sixty years. Its full realization could only be possible in a society where women enjoyed social and economic equality with men. We have not yet known such a society, but during this century we have moved a long way towards it. In my next talk I shall discuss this great social change, and some of its psychological consequences.

NOTES

1 The average daily population of all prisons in 1938 was 11,086, in 1961 29,025. *Report of the Commissioners of Prisons*, 1938 and 1961, H.M.S.O., Cmd. 6137 and Cmnd. 1798.

2 Particularly remarkable is the great increase in 'Crimes of Violence against the Person' from 1,583 convictions in 1938 to

11,519 convictions in 1961. Of these convictions youths under twenty-one accounted for 17·6 per cent. in 1938 and 41·0 per cent. in 1961. Home Office, *Criminal Statistics England and Wales*, H.M.S.O. 1961, Cmd. 1779.

See also Ministry of Education, *The Youth Service in England and Wales* (The Albemarle Report). H.M.S.O. 1960, Cmd. 929, pp. 16-17, and Ministry of Education, *15 to 18* (The Crowther Report), H.M.S.O., 1960, Vol. 1, pp. 40-42.

3 Llewellyn Smith, H. *New Survey of London Life and Labour.* London: P. S. King, 1930.

4 Mead, Margaret, *Coming of Age in Samoa.* New York: Morrow, 1928. London: Penguin Books, 1961.

5 An illustration of this process can be found in the way small boys view their fathers' occupations. An inquiry carried out with 13 to 14-year-old schoolboys showed that those from the secondary modern, as opposed to the grammar school, tended not only to aspire to the same work as their fathers, but to exaggerate the prestige and importance for society of these skilled and semi-skilled manual jobs. Himmelweit, H. T., Halsey, A. H. and Oppenheim, A. N. 'The Views of Adolescents on some Aspects of Social Class Structure', *Brit. J. Sociol.*, **3**, 148.

6 Erikson, E. H. 'Identity and the Life Cycle', *Psychological Issues*, Monograph No. 1. New York: Int. Univ. Press, 1959.

7 Wilkins, L. T. *Delinquent Generations*, A Home Office Research Unit Report, H.M.S.O., 1961.
Andry, R. G. *Delinquency and Parental Pathology.* London: Methuen, 1960. These British studies are in accordance with the findings of American workers; see
Glueck, S. & E. *Unravelling Juvenile Delinquency.* Boston: Harvard Univ. Press., 1950.

8 Gorer, G. *Exploring English Character.* London: Cresset Press, 1955, p. 170.

9 Tanner, J. M. *Education and Physical Growth.* London Univ. Press, 1961.

10 Mean Age at Marriage

		All Bachelors	All Spinsters
1901–05	. . .	26·9 years	25·4 years
1960	. . .	25·7 years	23·3 years

Registrar General. *Statistical Review of England and Wales for 1960*, Part II, 'Population', H.M.S.O., 1961.

11 Table on Legitimate Maternities by Duration of Marriage and Age at Marriage in:
Registrar General: *Statistical Review of England and Wales for 1960*, Part II, 'Population', H.M.S.O., 1961.

12 Theological correspondents have pointed out to me, since this lecture was delivered, that it was after all St Paul who wrote in his First Epistle to the Corinthians: 'And now abideth faith, hope and charity, these three; but the greatest of these is charity.' St Paul liked to have rules and regulations spelled out with precision; despite his abrupt conversion to Christianity he carried over into his new faith many of the conventions of his early religious upbringing, for example in his insistence that men must uncover their heads, and women cover theirs while at prayer (1 Corinthians 11) and that women should keep silence in churches (1 Corinthians 14). His views on sexual intercourse, and on the married state, were coloured by his belief that the Second Coming was imminent and that everyone would be well advised to remain celibate in anticipation of that event.

13 Booth, Charles. *Life and Labour of the People in London*. London, 1892–97.

14 Webb, Beatrice. *My Apprenticeship*. London: Longmans, 1926. Reprinted 1950.

15 London, Jack. *People of the Abyss*. London: Nelson, 1903. Reissued 1962.

16 Quoted in Jones, Ernest, *Sigmund Freud; Life and Work*. London: Hogarth Press, 1953, Vol. 1, p. 109.

17 Carstairs, G. M. *The Twice Born*. London: Hogarth Press, 1957. Indiana Univ. Press, 1958.

18 Ministry of Education, *15 to 18*, The Crowther Report 1960, Vol. I, pp. 118-19.
Ministry of Education, *Education in 1960*, H.M.S.O. 1961, Cmd. 1439.

19 Blishen E.: *Roaring Boys*. London: Thames & Hudson, 1955. 'The Last Refuge of Family Feeling', Chapter 8 in *The Human Sum*, ed. C. H. Rolph. London: Heinemann, 1957.

IV

THE CHANGING ROLE OF WOMEN

IV

The Changing Role of Women

The patterns of British family life today and at the beginning of this century are so different that one could easily regard them as belonging to two quite different societies. To some extent, of course, the differences are attributable to the widespread changes in our material environment; but the most striking changes—those I am concerned with now—are to be seen in the improved status of women, and in the changed relationships of husbands to wives, and of parents to children.

Three striking changes have transformed the pattern of women's domestic life: men and women now tend to marry earlier, to have much smaller families and to complete their families in a much shorter space of time. At the same time, women have benefited even more than men from the general increase in the expectation of life. When Professor Titmuss summarized these changes in one of his *Essays on the Welfare State*[1] he pointed out that at the beginning of this century a typical working-class mother devoted some fifteen years of her adult life to begetting and nursing her own children. She would expect to be preoccupied with raising her large family—and supervising her daughters' child-bearing—until she was nearing the end of her active life. Today, by the time a woman approaches forty, her youngest child is going to school; and at this age she can expect to live for another thirty-six years. She is ready to start a new career, and because of the increasing demand for female labour she has been able to do so. Industry, hitherto critical of the limitations of married women, has begun to accept these and adapt to them.[2]

Confronted with these major changes in women's life pattern, one, of course, wants to know what other changes they have entailed; one would certainly expect that men's behaviour had also changed. Sociological studies have shown how widespread are the changes of which many of us have first-hand knowledge. Husbands are now beginning to lend a hand with domestic tasks which used to be solely the wife's responsibility.

Less obvious, but of particular importance for the student of culture and personality, are the changes which are taking place in the whole concept of the roles of men and women in our society, in their mutual relationships and in the family settings in which their children will grow up.

Women have achieved greater social and political emancipation in Britain than in most European countries,[3] but their sexual emancipation is less evident than, for example, in Denmark or Sweden. There is a good deal of confusion and uncertainty, among both men and women, over the new roles of the sexes in our social life. Even in the professions, in business and in academic life where women have won acceptance on supposedly equal terms, one observes many instances of strain, of concealed embarrassment and of self-consciousness. In contrast with the situation in America, our career women do not yet feel at home in their new roles, nor are our men quite accustomed to working side by side with them.

I think it is worth stressing that, at the beginning of the century, ours was a frankly patriarchal society. Marriage was a very unequal partnership, in which all the social prestige went to the husband. This gave rise to a stereotype of the respective roles of men and women in which many tasks and interests were firmly labelled as manly, or as feminine pursuits, and most people in our society believed, as most people do in every society, that these conventions were dictated by laws of nature, or of God. In fact, however, anthropologists have shown that different cultures have prescribed very different rules for what men and women may and may not do.

The formal structure of the family differs, of course, widely in different societies. The only universal characteristics are the formalizing of adult sex relationships and of the protection and support of the mother and her young children. The mother's tie with her own infant is inevitably a basic feature, but her male support will take different forms in a household where one husband has several wives, in another where one wife is shared between several husbands, and in the quite numerous societies in which a woman looks to her brother and not to her husband for material and moral support.

While sex and childbearing are biological facts which are too stubborn to be denied, many other differences between men and women are dictated by social expectations much more than by biological realities. An important contribution of Freudian teaching has been the revelation that men and women are capable of sharing some of each other's psychological attributes. There is, in fact, a great deal of overlap between men and women in physical strength, aptitudes, temperament and interests. Some societies recognize this.[4] In these, men and women work side by side in the fields and at fishing; they share in the tasks of cooking and in the enjoyment of village feasts and dances. I found quite a lot of sharing of tasks among the Bhil tribe, with whom I lived for a time in India; many of their basic activities, such as cooking, herding cattle, gathering jungle produce were performed by both sexes and women sometimes took the initiative in the love affairs and elopements which were quite frequent occurrences among them.

There are some societies in which women do the heaviest work, while men conserve their energies for diplomacy, public eloquence or trading, and others in which women are confined to a strictly limited role. From the woman's point of view, it is not necessarily an advantage to be pampered. As an instance only, a colleague who has carried out numerous medical surveys in this country tells me that he has observed a suggestive correlation: in those few households which still maintain a retinue of servants, there is a strong tendency for the lady of the house to become an alcoholic.

Every stable society imposes rules of behaviour which inhibit the realization of some individual potentialities. This is compensated as a rule by the gratifications which only life in that society can provide. In times of social change, however, this equilibrium tends to become upset, and when this happens conformity to social norms can be maintained only by subjecting some individuals to considerable stress, and causing many of them to break down. At such times, the study of those who fall sick can contribute to a better understanding of these points of social stress.

Professor Lee, a psychologist, encountered just such a situation a few years ago when he set out to study a curious epidemic of prolonged crying fits which developed among the Zulu women in South Africa at the end of last century, and which now affects nearly half the women of the[5] tribe. At first he was told that the cause was obvious; this was a people in which many of the men went away to work in the gold mines, so presumably it was their wives who responded to the disruption of their lives in this dramatic fashion—but he soon found that screaming fits occurred just as often in the wives of men who did *not* leave home. In the end he found that the fits were associated with resentment against their role of servitude in a male-dominated society on the part of women who had only recently been introduced to new roles and customs which were at variance with the old tribal traditions. The interesting thing was that the women who had fits of screaming had not yet reached the stage of consciously recognizing this resentment, although it found expression in their dreams and in their responses to personality tests to a significantly greater degree than in those of their more adaptable sisters.

Nearer home, we have had a number of similar, if less dramatic, indications of conflict between women's domestic and their social roles; nor is it only the women who complain.

Reference is often made to the figures for divorce as a sign of social disorganization: but this is to take an oversimplified view. Divorce is admittedly a confession of failure, but it is not necessarily an unrelieved disaster.

Many primitive peoples invoke supernatural sanctions against adultery, but most societies make formal provision for divorce and remarriage. In our own society until the present century the Church made divorce very difficult indeed; and as a result the victims of failed marriages lived embittered and love-less lives. We have to remember that never before in the history of our race have the words 'till death us do part' carried the implication of so many years of married life as they do now.

Doctors have long been aware of the frequency of neurotic ill-health among young and middle-aged married women, who attend their surgeries and hospital out-patient departments with many vague complaints: if they have anything in common, it is that they feel tired and are unhappy. More than twenty years ago Lord Taylor gave this syndrome the name of 'suburban neurosis'.[6] He pointed out that it was most prevalent among active women whose children were growing up, and whose household duties were no longer demanding. It was, in fact, a reaction on their part to the feeling of useless-ness. Lord Taylor noticed that when an emergency arose in their homes, when their husband or child fell ill, their symp-toms were forgotten in the satisfaction of finding that they were needed by someone.

The coming of old age does something to redress the balance. Then, it is the husband who finds himself idle and useless, while his wife's role continues and may be enhanced when a reduced income puts her thrift and domestic efficiency at a premium.

Statistical evidence confirms that elderly married women are less prone than women who are single or widowed to suffer from depression[7]; on the other hand, of all groups in the community it is elderly men, whether married or single, who contribute most to the annual total of suicides.[8]

In our society, surveys of neurotic illness have consistently shown that women are more prone to these complaints than men[9]; and yet this is surprising, because in general women are the tougher sex, better able to endure pain, and certainly out-living men by several years. It seems reasonable to associate their apparent susceptibility to emotional disorders with the internal conflicts which they experience in their day-to-day existence.

The so-called 'suburban neurosis' is due to society's having failed to provide a constructive role for these mothers. Their sense of uselessness, of having no worthwhile contribution to make, was the precipitating factor in their illness, but the fact that they fell ill with symptoms of depression and hypo-chondriasis could be attributed to their own personalities which left them vulnerable to this kind of collapse. Other young wives, in the same circumstances, find that their Achilles' heel lies in a tendency to be overwhelmed by unreasoning fear: such women often find themselves giving way to sudden attacks of panic while travelling in a bus, or being in a crowded shop. In many cases this leads them to restrict their activities more and more until they may become completely house-bound. Their distress is aggravated by the fact that they them-selves regard these fears as irrational and unwarranted, and yet they cannot overcome them; often they begin to fear that they are going out of their minds.

These patients, no less than the crying Zulu wives, are in the grip of emotional forces of which they are not consciously aware. In order to help them, it is not sufficient (nor even always necessary) to unravel the infantile origins of their neurosis—after all, until this illness they may have been func-tioning reasonably well as wives and mothers. It *is* essential, however, to help them to recognize the real factors which upset their emotional balance, so that they can take steps to relieve their situation.

An important consequence of the attitudes towards sexuality which dominated British life in late Victorian times, and which still has a lingering influence, was the remarkable frequency of frigidity in married women. Popular views about the physical aspect of sex relationships, as handed down from mother to daughter, tended to emphasize that only men and beasts really enjoyed intercourse, whereas women had to learn to endure it. This teaching coupled with dire warnings about the hardships of pregnancy and childbirth effectively prevented many women from experiencing a satisfactory sex life; and often its baleful influence was reinforced by narrow religious dogmatism. Our Churches have lent themselves all too readily, in the past, to denigrating sensual, and especially sexual enjoyment; and yet the basic Christian emphasis upon respect for the individual personality of every man and woman provides the best possible starting-point for the new and more equal relationship between man and wife which our society is now trying to develop.

Women have not been the only casualties of Victorian middle-class attitudes towards sex. There have also been some men whose sexual development remained incomplete or deviant because of terrifying fantasies engendered by the secrecy and shame with which these matters were surrounded in so many respectable British families.

More extreme disruptions of normal behaviour are found in the psychoses. For a few unfortunate women, childbirth precipitates severe mental illness. In trying to understand these illnesses, as in the case of severe depression occurring after the change of life, we have to consider the role of changes in the balance of sex hormones circulating in the blood; but we should be very short-sighted if we failed to recognize the emotional significance of child-bearing and of the end of child-bearing respectively for these women. In a psychotic illness the sensible, rational self is temporarily in abeyance; bizarre and at times horrible fantasies enter into consciousness and may be acted out—the distracted mother may even have to be restrained from killing her own child. A puerperal psychosis can be a nightmare experience; and yet this nightmare only reveals fantasies which all of us may harbour, although safely repressed in our unconscious minds. Sometimes it is the father who becomes carried away by psychotic fantasies which are the obverse of his normal feelings; there are occasional tragic cases, unintelligible and shocking merely to read of in the newspapers, where a man may kill his wife and children before taking his own life.

My point in drawing attention to these cases of acute failure and distress is to show that though our society has taken steps to ensure that psychotic parents both receive treatment and are protected from the consequences of their acts, we have remained relatively incurious about the emotional forces which underlie these illnesses. It is not sufficient to say that these unfortunates have gone mad. The real challenge is to explain why they should go mad in just this way. Here Freudian psychology is not so helpful; its concern has been with the remote origins, rather than the immediate precipitants of mental breakdown. Instead we must turn to social psychology, to seek more light on the interactions, and the mutual expectations of man and wife in the testing crises of their married life.

I have found that certain of Jung's concepts make these sudden catastrophes more readily intelligible. Like Freud, he believed that most mental illnesses are due to a disintegration of consciousness caused by the irresistible invasion of unconscious contents; but Jung maintained that while we all exhibit a public personality (our *persona*, or mask) we also carry within us not only our private conscious self but also a sinister aspect of our own nature which he called the *shadow*. As in the story of Dr Jekyll and Mr Hyde, the shadow contains all the fierce, immoral urges which are the obverse of our waking aspirations; it is these elements which break out when the cohesion of the normal personality is temporarily lost.

Jung believed that every person's unconscious mind contained elements contrary, yet complementary to his conscious make-up; he thought that people who are emotionally close to one another, such as a child and his parent, or man and wife, often perceive and respond to the other's unconscious rather than to his conscious self. Serious troubles can arise when this symmetrical arrangement of conscious and unconscious personality traits breaks down and, for example, a mother's normal life becomes subject to promptings from her unconscious. To some extent, this happens to us all—we are seldom quite as reasonable as we would like to believe—but a few people become so much affected by these impulses that one can't help noticing glaring discrepancies between what they intend and what they actually do.

The child of such a parent finds himself repeatedly caught in a 'double bind', that is in a situation in which he is given simultaneous but mutually contradictory cues, so that whatever he does will be wrong. It has been plausibly argued that children brought up by such a parent become predisposed to schizophrenic breakdown[10]; but this hypothesis cannot be verified until methods have been devised to demonstrate this 'double bind' in action and to measure the frequency of its occurrence in normal families, and in families in which a child is becoming schizophrenic.

Psychotic illness represents the complete breakdown of social functioning. It occurs when biological, social and emotional events combine to make it impossible for an individual to maintain the coherence of his personality (and this happens to some people in every society).

Neurotic illness is a more sensitive indicator of the new stresses which occur in a period of rapid social change. During recent years, in which our society has been trying to work out new roles for men and women, certain psychological gains and losses have begun to make themselves apparent.

On the positive side, the abandonment of the old, rather rigid definitions of male and female roles has made it possible for us to recognize and give expression to the feminine aspects of man's nature, and the masculine element in woman. There have always been some men so constituted, or so biased by their early experiences, that they can only feel strongly in a homosexual relationship. We have no reason to believe that the number of homosexuals is any greater in our society today than it was in 1895, when Oscar Wilde was tried; but there is no doubt that public opinion is less alarmed, less vengeful now than it was then.

In fact, women are being asked to play roles which are as yet, in our society, in conflict. Society has not yet abandoned the Victorian ideal of the fully-domesticated mother and wife, destined to find her satisfactions only through service for others. Because of this lingering conception, remorselessly perpetuated by all women's magazines, women are still made to feel guilty if they seek for themselves satisfactions which come from the fulfilment of their own peculiar talents and potentialities. Because society still does not accept them on equal terms with men, such women are forced to manifest an aggressiveness which is not an inherent prerequisite of the job they perform but only of the social situation in which they find themselves. Conscious often themselves that this assertiveness is not the best foundation for their relationship with husband and children, they are at the same time made to feel profoundly guilty by a society which categorizes them as rejecting mothers. At the same time, men, who have begun to accept the equality of men and women as a fact of life in our community today, show a readiness to turn over some of the less congenial of *their* traditional parental duties; women are being asked to shoulder new responsibilities (such as control of the family budget, disciplining of the children) at the same time as they are being helped with the traditionally feminine household tasks of washing up, child minding and so on.

Resentful of the stresses imposed by their new liberty, resentful and frustrated by the restriction placed on this liberty by the years of child-bearing; anxious and guilty at this resentment, uncertain even of the division of parental responsibilities, such women begin to doubt whether femininity is indeed compatible with all the variety of roles they must play.

Perhaps the greatest strain which present-day marriages have to undergo is the acceptance by husbands of their wives' new problems, and the need for them to help their wives to lead more active and more satisfying lives. This may be at the cost of some inconvenience, and may require men to a further sacrifice of their feeling of importance; its reward will come in the happier relationships which may prevail when wives are no longer so harassed and irritable. The first step, however, is to recognize their present plight. Already a hundred years ago, Florence Nightingale put this very well when she wrote: 'Men are irritated with women for not being happy. They take it as a personal offence.'

American women, to whom equality with men in education and in work is a greater reality than it is here, are ahead of us in resolving these difficulties. Because they are freely accepted as colleagues in all areas of activity, American women do not need to doubt that they can be feminine *and* share in these roles. But because their career expectations are greater, they suffer more from the enforced inactivity, seclusion and frustrations of the child-bearing period. Irritability and depression are prominent features of their complaints—a syndrome which New York physicians have christened 'Mrs Hillside' after a prosperous dormitory suburb.

As the new concept of marriage takes shape, in which young people look forward to married life as a mutually satisfying physical and personal relationship, women are becoming dissatisfied when these expectations are not fulfilled.

Women, nearly twice as often as men, are brought to hospital after attempting suicide.[11] Many of these incidents can be regarded as a dramatic protest against a painful situation, rather than as a serious attempt to end their lives. Among the numerous personal reasons which provoke such incidents, quite the commonest is marital disharmony. Sometimes this is the sign of a breaking marriage; but sometimes the dramatic gesture of distress has the desired effect of stimulating a more intense and considerate relationship.[12]

Men have usually been quick to complain if the physical side of their marriage proved unsatisfactory, no doubt because sexual potency is the criterion of manhood. Now, however, women also are beginning to recognize their marriage as incomplete if it does not give them physical as well as emotional satisfaction. For some men this in turn presents a frightening challenge; many of them find themselves obscurely impelled to prove their virility by exposing themselves to strangers or to little girls. Indecent exposure has become one of the commonest sexual offences in our cities; the men who do this often claim to be happily married but almost invariably they are found to be weak and insecure in their capacity as husbands.[13]

This is a time when women are taking the lead in re-exploring and re-discovering their own nature, and, in so doing, modifying our concept of man's nature also. They have compelled us to think carefully whether we really mean it when we men claim to regard them as different but equal; no less human, no less an individual, and no less important than ourselves. Our society has never yet embodied this assumption in its institutions, but during the present century we have taken several steps in this direction, and this has led to a series of personal readjustments in which probably every family in this island is to some extent involved.

72

NOTES

1 Titmuss, R. M. *Essays on the Welfare State* (Chapter 5: The Position of Women). London: Allen & Unwin, 1958. New Haven: Yale Univ. Press, 1959. see also:
Myrdal, A. and Klein, V. *Women's Two Roles*. London: Routledge & Kegan Paul, 1956.

2 Jephcott, Pearl. *Married Women Working*. London: Allen & Unwin, 1962.

3 The following are some of the milestones in this process of social emancipation:

(*a*) Property Rights.

1882. The Married Women's Property Act gave women the right to own and dispose of their own property, and themselves to enter into contracts in respect of such property.

(*b*) Political Rights.

1918. The Representation of the People Act, granted the franchise to most women over thirty.

1919. The Qualification of Women Act admitted women as members of the House of Commons and in this year Viscountess Astor became the first woman M.P.

1928. Women of twenty-one were enfranchised on equal terms with men.

1958. Life Peerages Act—under this Act men and women equally could be admitted as life members of the House of Lords. Four women took their seat in this year.

1963. A proposed Bill would give women the right to sit as hereditary members of the House of Lords.

(*c*) Professional Rights.

The Sex Disqualification (Removal) Act, 1919.

Many professions, principally the law, were opened to women by this Act. The first woman was called to the Bar in 1922, but only in 1962 was the first woman appointed a County Court Judge. The higher branches of the Diplomatic Service were not opened to women until 1946.

In 1954 the principle of equal pay for women was conceded

THIS ISLAND NOW

to civil servants, and the gradual introduction is now almost accomplished.

(d) Matrimonial Rights.

The Matrimonial Causes Act, 1923, gave women the right to sue for divorce on the grounds of their husband's adultery, cruelty or desertion no longer being additionally necessary.

4 See, for instance:
Mead, Margaret. *Male and Female* (Chapter 8: Rhythm of Work and Play). New York: Morrow, 1952. London: Gollancz, 1950.

5 Lee, S. G. McK. *Stress and Adaptation* (Inaugural Lecture delivered at the University of Leicester on 23rd Nov., 1961). Leicester University Press, 1962.

6 Taylor, S. 'Suburban Neurosis', *Lancet*, **i**, 759, 1938.

7 Ødegard, O. 'New Data on Marriage and Mental Disease: The Incidence of Psychoses in the Widowed and Divorced', *J. ment. Sci.*, Vol. **99**, No. 417, Oct. 1953.

8 Sainsbury, P. *Suicide in London*. London: Maudsley Monograph No. 1, 1955.
Sainsbury, P. 'Suicide in Old Age', *Proc. R. Soc. Med.*, **54**, 266.

9 Kessel, W. I. N. and Shepherd, M. 'Neurosis in Hospital and General Practice', *J. ment. Sci.*, Vol. **108**, No. 453, Mar., 1962.
Shepherd, M. and Gruenberg, E. M. *Millbank Memorial Fund Qtly*, Vol. **35**, p. 258.

10 Bateson, G., Jackson, D. D., Haley, J. and Weakland, J. H. 'Toward a Theory of Schizophrenia', *Behav. Sci.*, **1**, 251, 1956.
Bateson, G. 'Minimal Requirements for a Theory of Schizophrenia', *A.M.A. Arch. gen. Psychiat.*, **2**, 477, 1960.

11 Stengel, E. and Cook, N. G. *Attempted Suicide*. Maudsley Monograph No. 4, 1, 1958. London: Chapman & Hall.

12 Kessel, W. I. N. and McCulloch, W. Research in progress on Social Factors in Attempted Suicide, M.R.C. Unit, Department of Psychological Medicine, University of Edinburgh.

13 Rosen, I. Chapter in: *The Pathology and Treatment of Sexual Deviation, A Methodological Approach*, Ed., I. Rosen. London: Oxford Univ. Press, 1963.

V

'LIVING AND PARTLY LIVING'

V

'Living and Partly Living'

People have always found it easy to believe that life in their time was much more stressful than that of previous generations. As far as physical distress is concerned, today most of the killing diseases of early adult life as of childhood have been mastered. Many more of us now can expect to survive into our sixties and seventies. But surprisingly in the last hundred years, there has been very little prolongation of the limits of our active life. Even now, among working men in their early sixties, one man in ten finds himself incapacitated by sickness for three months out of each year.[1] For more than a century many writers (both medical and lay) have attributed the increase of mental illness in our society to the ever-increasing pace of modern life. One hundred years ago, for example, a writer to *The Times* confidently ascribed the increase in the number of the insane to 'the rapid and frequent railway travelling of this age' which, he argued 'must be injurious to the brain'.

As yet, however, careful inquiries have not been able to demonstrate a real increase in serious mental illness—at any rate in persons under fifty—during the last century. Whether the minor forms of mental illness—the neuroses, obsessional states and personality disorders—have been increasing we cannot say with any confidence because we have no reliable estimates of their prevalence in earlier times. What we can say, however, is that they have become much more widely recognized and discussed, and that patients are now much readier than before to seek help for these complaints. Many more people in Britain consult psychiatrists today than ever before—but this is partly because never before have there been so many psychiatrists to consult. It is also true that general physicians are rediscovering the importance of emotional disturbance in the origin of many minor physical complaints. I say rediscovering, because these concepts were well known to some physicians of the seventeenth and eighteenth centuries. George Cheyne, who gave his name to Cheyne Walk in Chelsea, maintained that a third of all his patients were neurotic: in his book *The English Disease*, published in 1733, he wrote that the English were especially prone to nervous disorders. Neurosis, therefore, has long been prevalent in our society—as it is to some degree in every society. In times of rapid social change many people find a need for reassurance, which traditionally has been met by invoking supernatural help through the agency of priests or witch-doctors. In the developing towns of West Africa, for example, magical cults and healing shrines have multiplied in the last few years.[2] Here in Britain we are more sophisticated: we take tranquillizers—but we often take them with magical expectations. Before discussing these drugs, however, I should like to draw attention to two allied conditions, namely suicide and depression; these present an especial challenge to society because each represents an individual's sense of despair of life's having any meaning.

Suicide has for many years been of special interest to sociologists, not only because it expresses such unequivocal repudiation of social values, but perhaps especially because it is a social phenomenon which can be counted. For well over a hundred years it has been known that suicide rates differ in different societies and that they persist with remarkable regularity from year to year so long as no major social change occurs.

Durkheim, the pioneer of empirical research in sociology, devoted years of study to this topic.[3] He was concerned to show why, during a century marked by great material progress, the suicide rate increased in almost every European country. His analysis still has relevance for us today.

Durkheim pointed out that suicides were sometimes altruistic, in that the individual surrendered his life for the greater good of the family, group or community to which he belonged; other suicides were egoistic, prompted not by concern for others but by a purely individual despair; others again were prompted by what he called *anomie*, that is the loss of social cohesion, of the sense of shared social sentiments and values. And it was the egoistic and the anomic types of suicide which had shown a tendency to increase. In discussing their social causes, Durkheim pointed out that as modern industrial society changed from being dominated by tradition and religion, to become a rational and secular state, many of the former mainstays of social stability were undermined. It is interesting to recall his two criteria for social advance: one was the replacement of traditionalism by rational understanding and deliberate choice; the other, an extension of self-interest from the individual or a local group to recognition of the common interest of a larger community.

Durkheim's concern was exclusively with society. He recognized that social institutions must have an influence on individuals' lives, but he did not believe that knowledge of individual psychology could contribute to a better understanding of these institutions themselves. This was perhaps because in his day there was no adequate psychology of human motivation. His influence is still strong in sociological thought, not only because he set a pattern for empirical research, but because the great issues he contended with—those of *anomie*, that is, loss of social cohesion, and of the necessity for exercising deliberate choice—are very much alive today. One finds *anomie* exemplified in many studies of social disorganization; and the insistence upon choice (if not Durkheim's faith in the triumph of rationality) is echoed in contemporary existentialist philosophy.

Since Durkheim died in 1916, there has been a further development of the trends in society which he described—a further weakening of religion, of traditional values, of social hierarchies, of extended family ties. The old forms persist, but they are emptied of much of their significance: they no longer provide fixed points for the orientation of social values.

Durkheim hoped that a new basis, to replace tradition and religion as the source of moral judgments, might be provided by groups of people engaged in a common occupation. This prophecy has been fulfilled, but in a way different from what he expected.

In his book *The Organization Man*, William H. Whyte[4] has shown the extent to which the growth of vast business corporations has come to provide a whole sub-culture, an enveloping mode of life in which conformity to the organization's norms and suppression of individuality become matters of supreme importance. The alarming thing about this situation is the docility with which young men seem prepared to sacrifice their individuality in exchange for the prospect of financial security in an organization.

Another American sociologist, David Riesman,[5] has contrasted three types of moral systems—those which are *tradition-centred* (as in the Middle Ages, when religious and autocratic authority were unchallenged), those which are *inner-directed*, each man obeying his own conscience and claiming direct access to his God (as in the Protestant ethic); and thirdly those which are *other-directed*, in which the individual subordinates his own values to the expectations of the other people who surround him. The state of *other-direction*, which Riesman finds increasingly common in modern society, encourages feelings of individual insignificance; it also causes a spiritual emptiness which leaves men susceptible to irrational demagogic ideologies. Other-directedness reflects an impoverishment of the personality.

Conformity to the Organization and submission to other-direction; both accept a recognition of social bonds; both are consonant with conventional, if debased, middle-class values.

If the picture which Richard Hoggart[6] has drawn for us of contemporary working-class society is accurate—and it certainly rings true—then for the majority of our fellow-citizens even these meagre values have very little meaning.

Hoggart has surveyed the life and leisure of today's urban working class in order to appraise what our nation has gained as a consequence of the relatively new phenomenon of universal literacy. His findings are dismal. Elementary schooling has taught our population to read, but it falls short of imparting an appreciation of literature or art; it develops a dim awareness of scientific progress, but fails to equip the ordinary man with the wish, or the ability, to go on learning for himself. As a result he vacillates between total scepticism towards all values which are not crudely materialistic and extreme credulity for assertions which invoke the name of science. Hoggart reports the withering away of verbal traditions, of local activities in which working people used to take part. In their place he sees the spread of a faceless culture whose members passively imbibe the endless stream of trivial, intellectually enervating entertainments offered to them by the mass media.

It is in Hoggart's faceless culture of our imperfectly literate masses, rather than in the more sophisticated world of the Organization Man that we can recognize the loss of social cohesion, the loss of the sense of shared social sentiments and values in our society. In his study, as in any sociological analysis, the behaviour of groups of people provides the ultimate observation. But when one meets them as individuals it is no longer possible to remain altogether dispassionate and detached. To encounter a fellow human being in a state of despair compels one to share, at least in imagination, his elemental problems: Is there any meaning in life? Is there any point in his staying alive?

During this year over 5,000 people will have committed suicide in Britain: at a conservative estimate, another 30,000 will have attempted suicide, and many thousands more will have lived through—or are still contending with—a state of depression in which life becomes a pointless misery. Apart from those who are seriously depressed there are many more who lead a lack-lustre existence, 'living and partly living'; and there are others whose dissatisfaction with life bursts out in acts of violence. A smouldering sense of defeat sometimes can break out in this way. Murder is not infrequently followed by the suicide of the murderer; but this association is found more often in the suicides of poor people than in those of the better-off. If there is this aggressive accompaniment of melancholia, may there not be an element of depression and despair behind the increasing number of violent crimes in our society. One of the inescapable, and still unexplained, realities of life in this island now is the recent recrudescence of violence which reversed the trend of the previous hundred years, and which has contributed to the almost threefold increase in our prison population since 1938.[7] Why is it that grown men and women, no less than teenagers, are registering this unmistakable vote of no confidence in a society which has in so many ways improved their physical and material conditions of life?

I believe the answer is to be found in our loss of conviction in any supra-personal system of values, which would lend significance both to the existence of our species, and to our individual lives.

Until this century, for the majority of our race the ultimate criterion of man's significance was held to be his direct relationship with God. 'What is man's chief end?' asks the Scottish Shorter Catechism, and gives the reply: 'Man's chief end is to glorify God and to enjoy Him forever'. This theme is reiterated in other Christian teachings, and in many other religions.

In our society there are, of course, still some people who sincerely believe in the teachings of the Christian Church, but the Church's own statistics show that they have become a minority group—a rather small minority.[8] The rituals of the Church persist—some of them, such as the practice of infant baptism, with remarkable tenacity—but one suspects that they are often mere forms, as empty of significance as the habit of touching wood for luck. Most people today lack religious conviction: in its place there persists a left-over jumble of ethical precepts, now bereft of their significance, and the widespread habit of occasional private prayer to a God in whom most people only half believe.

The confusion which prevails in popular thinking about the concepts of determinism and personal responsibility contributes to this partial eclipse of moral values. By showing how often our apparently deliberate actions are in fact determined by motives of which we are unaware, psycho-analysis has undermined our confidence in the reality of free will.

It is a curious anomaly that Freud both postulated complete determinism in man's psychic life and at the same time made it his aim in treatment to extend the area of conscious control over one's own activities. In fact, however, Freud's teaching was much more successful in exposing former illusions of free will than it was in helping ordinary people to come to terms with the problems of existence. It seems somehow paradoxical that the virtues which were manifested in his personal life were the legacy, not of his own discoveries about human nature, but of his tacit acceptance of Hebraic morality together with the traditions of stoic philosophy. Freud had the moral stamina to remain completely agnostic; but he was sustained by the quite unreasoning conviction which enabled him to say: 'I consider ethics to be self-explanatory. . . . Actually, I have never done a mean thing.'[9] Few people can sustain this double burden of agnosticism and rectitude.

At this point it is necessary to pause for a moment to ask whether these problems of violence and unhappiness and feelings of insignificance can properly be regarded as of medical or

83

psychiatric concern. We were all indeed compelled to pause three years ago when Lady Wootton threw down her challenge in her clearly argued book *Social Science and Social Pathology*.[10] In her view, the uninformed public was becoming too readily persuaded that psychiatry held the key to the understanding of antisocial behaviour. She poured scorn on psychiatric social workers who, in the absence of irrefutable evidence, appear to believe that psychotherapy will have a good effect upon delinquents. And yet, being scrupulously fair, she presented the positive evidence (so far as it goes) which has been advanced in support of theories about the psychological origins of crime and abnormality. For example, after demonstrating flaws of logic and of research method in several reports of the ill effects suffered by children deprived of their mothers' care she concluded: 'Now and again their deprivation seems to express itself in a well-marked pattern of indifference to everybody except themselves, of which one of the expressions is repeated stealing. More than this however we cannot say.'[11]

Research workers in this field would acknowledge that her remarks are just, and expressed with true scientific caution; but they are engaged in further studies which will, they hope, enable them to say a little more about these phenomena.

I believe it is important for us to be clear in our own minds about the limits of psychiatric competence. A great deal of medicine has to be practised on the basis of purely empirical discoveries, or of hypotheses which have not yet been definitely proved. It is the doctor's responsibility to keep in mind the tentative nature of much of his knowledge of disease, but it is certainly not his business to share this intellectual uncertainty with his patient—on the contrary, he must impart the conviction that he is treating the disease with the most effective means available. He knows that his conviction of the appropriateness of what he is doing is itself an important part of his treatment because it arouses the patient's confidence and his will to recover. Owing to the large areas of uncertainty in psychiatric and psycho-analytic theory, this weighing of intellectual doubt against therapeutic assurance is particularly important in this field: therapies which rely upon the active involvement of the personality of the therapist demand his unreserved commitment if they are to prove themselves effective; and yet the therapist must be able periodically to withdraw from his involvement in order objectively to assess and to evaluate what has been going on, if he is to succeed in turning this art into a science.

In this respect, psychiatry is not alone but shares the obligations common to all the social sciences, and especially those which are involved in social planning. It is easier to recognize social evils than to fathom their origins or to treat them. Where our understanding is imperfect, treatment itself should be regarded as an experiment, and this is where I find myself at variance with Lady Wootton. Certainly psychiatrists must be modest in their claims, knowing the limitations of their sure knowledge; and yet, confronted with the scale of human mental suffering, we have no right *not* to try such techniques of healing as we possess. Here it is surely legitimate to act upon a promising hypothesis provided that we do so in such a way that the results of our treatment or intervention will contribute towards the confirmation, or the rebuttal, or the modification of that hypothesis.

In my opinion, the most neglected field in medical science today is the psychological study (along experimental lines) of mental disorders and their treatment. In saying this, I am well aware of my professional bias. I am aware, too, that psychotherapists have been making similar assertions since the beginning of this century; and yet in Britain at least very little attention has been paid to them—least of all in our great schools of medicine. During recent years however many physicians and even more general practitioners have become aware of the size of the medical and social problems presented by patients with troubled minds, and they have begun to lend support to the call for more research to be applied to these baffling complaints. All too often, however, they seem to think only in terms of brain disease, as though a person's mind could be treated as simply as his liver.

Perhaps nowhere in contemporary society can we see such clear evidence of the persistence of magical thinking as in the doctor's willingness to be persuaded (well, half-persuaded) that the drug houses have newly discovered the elixir of life. In recent years extravagant hopes have been centred upon the psychotropic drugs, drugs which will relieve agitation and depression, and others which calm the turmoil of the acutely deranged. These drugs are often effective, if only for a time; but they have been used so intemperately that we still know remarkably little about their scope and limitations and their possible dangers; and yet they are being prescribed today in their millions.

I do not want to deny the help that these drugs have brought to many seriously ill patients, but only to point out that when they are taken to relieve the emotional distress caused by problems of living they are merely anodyne, and offer no lasting solution.

Even considerable physical discomfort becomes bearable when it is found to have a meaning and a limit. On the other hand neurotic distress is greatest when it appears to be incomprehensible. To allay the symptom while failing to explore, and if possible eradicate, the cause has always been bad medicine. Why then have we tolerated it so long where neurotic illness is concerned?

Some people assert that psychological methods of investigation and treatment have been justifiably spurned, because they have never been objectively tested and proved to be superior to simpler remedies. This is a legitimate criticism, and one which is now being met; but one cannot help noticing that similar considerations did not prevent doctors all over the world from employing costly, laborious and sometimes dangerous physical treatments like insulin coma and brain surgery upon many thousands of mentally ill patients, only to discover many years later that these procedures were of very limited efficacy indeed.

No, it is not on logical grounds that medicine has so long resisted psychotherapy. I believe that here we have another instance of events (in this case the series of discoveries about the workings of the human mind which were initiated by Sigmund Freud) that outstripped the grasp of human imagination. We have been living in an era dominated by discoveries in biology and in the physical sciences, discoveries which have brought tremendous changes in our material surroundings. Medicine too has profited from these discoveries, and is even now on the verge of acquiring new knowledge about the origin and transmission of life, the processes of ageing and of cancer, and, we hope, of the biological processes involved in mental illness: but I believe that as a result medicine has become too exclusively preoccupied with material techniques, techniques which are appropriate to biochemistry, or pharmacology or experimental biology, but which are far from being the only valid means of studying the human mind. Even in the practical realm of treating the sick, it may well be that the great upsurge of biological research has already made its major contribution.

Meanwhile we are neglecting some of the greatest health problems of our contemporary society, the problems of faulty psychological and social adjustment. In the history of human thought key ideas have sometimes been seized upon at once, at other times have had to wait for centuries before they could receive practical application—Democritus' theory of the atom is a case in point. Freud himself, surprised by the vehemence with which his theories were at first denounced, said that this was because his ideas disturbed the sleep of the world. I believe that it is time that our society awakened to the need for clearer self-knowledge as a means to remedying some of the current disorders in our private and our public life.

NOTES

1 Data provided by Professor J. N. Morris, to be published in his book *Uses of Epidemiology* (2nd Edition, in preparation). Edinburgh: Livingstone.

2 Balandier, G. *Afrique Ambiguë*. Paris: Plon, 1959.
  Field, Margaret. *Search for Security*. London: Faber & Faber, 1960.

3 Durkheim, E. *Le Suicide*. Paris, 1897. English translation, *Suicide*. Routledge & Kegan Paul, London: 1952. Chicago: Free Press, 1951.

4 Whyte, W. H. *The Organization Man*. New York: Simon & Schuster, 1956. Penguin Books, 1960.

5 Riesman, D. *The Lonely Crowd*. New Haven: Yale Univ. Press, 1950.

6 Hoggart, R. *The Uses of Literacy*. London: Chatto & Windus, 1957. Penguin Books, 1958.

7 See Note 1, Lecture 3.

8 The number of Easter communicants fell from 94 in 1901 to 68 in 1958 per 1,000 of the population aged fifteen or over. This and other statistics on church-going are given in:
  Statistical Unit of the Central Board of Finance of the Church of England: *Facts and Figures about the Church of England*. London: Church House, 1962.

9 Quoted in Jones, E. *Sigmund Freud, Life and Work*. London: Hogarth Press, Vol. III, 1957, p. 264. New York: Basic Books, 1957, p. 247.

10 Wootton, Lady. *Social Science and Social Pathology*. London: Allen & Unwin, 1959.

11 Wootton, Lady, *Ibid.*, p. 156.

VI

THE CHANGING BRITISH CHARACTER

VI

The Changing British Character

A little over a hundred years ago, at the opening of the Great Exhibition of 1851, Prince Albert said: 'We are living in a period of most wonderful transition, which tends rapidly to accomplish that great end to which all history points—the realization of the unity of mankind.'[1]

His words—lofty, vague, optimistic—conjure up a picture of what we were like (or rather, of what our ruling classes were like) in the middle of Queen Victoria's reign. For a time, as our Empire spread round the world, it was possible to imagine the whole of mankind united under the beneficent rule of British gentlemen. Then we were the richest country in the world, although these riches were based upon poverty, disease and misery on a scale which we would now find intolerable.

The contrast with the cultural climate of today would be most apparent in three respects: in those days, glaring social inequalities were accepted; there was a complacent belief in human progress of which our society was the highest embodiment; and the Church had a powerful influence in public life. And yet already, in the second half of last century, counter-forces were at work. The Labour movement began to take shape, Darwinism shattered our complacency about human superiority, and the Church, by tending to support the established order and reject scientific discoveries, alienated both the common man and many intellectuals.

During this century we have learned to reject authority, or at any rate to challenge those who claim authority to produce evidence to validate their claims. This happened with religion first, with medicine rather later, and it may well be the turn of the law next. The great debate between Herbert Spencer, T. H.

Huxley and the Bishops ended in a defeat for religious dogmatism, but it can also be seen to have helped the Church to redefine its proper sphere of authority. In medicine, the new generation of scientifically trained doctors demand rigorous standards of verification: some of our most eminent physicians are shocked to discover that the weight of their personal opinion is no longer considered a sufficient support for their clinical pronouncements. The next field to be influenced by the demand for verification may well be the law: perhaps even Judges are not infallible. There is talk of research on the range of sentences which are imposed for apparently similar crimes, and on the comparative effects of different forms of punishment on the criminal's subsequent behaviour.

The realization of the fallibility of personal opinion, and of the need for experimental testing of received ideas, has altered the way we look at many of the social problems which I mentioned in previous talks. We no longer set out with the assumption that we know which institutions are harmful. Instead, we approach problems such as crime, or promiscuity or alcoholism by first trying to understand them more fully. We begin by observing the situation as objectively as possible with the aim of identifying the social antecedents of particular events or patterns of behaviour. Value-judgments still have to be made before we decide upon any form of intervention; but nowadays these value-judgments are seldom couched in terms of absolutes. Rather, we state our reasons for saying that under these particular circumstances a particular change is desirable. By limiting and defining our intentions in this way, we make it easier to measure the success or failure of a given intervention.

It may seem that in these talks I have dwelt too much on the black side, shown myself to be too preoccupied with social and individual pathology. Perhaps it is because I am a clinician that my attention keeps returning to the indicators of malaise; but social scientists, too, are notoriously more interested in studying situations of crisis and stress than tranquil, smoothly functioning institutions. One reason, of course, is that like the clinician they are never invited to interfere with a successful institution.

Just for a moment, let me consider this unfamiliar exercise: how would I start to describe the positive achievements of our society? First, I should have to declare my criteria. Following Durkheim, I should count it a gain wherever rational judgment, rather than emotion or rigid dogmatism determined public decisions; and also a gain whenever the narrow self-interest of individuals or local groups gave way to an acceptance of the common interest of a larger community. In the field of psychology, my criterion for social advance would be the accessibility, for everyone in our community, of the means to develop their innate capabilities.

This last sounds an extravagant idea. In our diversified and complex society we fairly readily acquire certain skills and certain types of specialized knowledge at the expense of renouncing many others; but there are some other attributes of personality which also require to be developed, and which would enhance us all, and yet we have never yet been able to make their development possible for the majority in our society. These rarer attributes include intellectual curiosity, tolerance and consideration for others, spontaneous emotional responsiveness to people and to ideas, and aesthetic taste and creativity.

As a nation, we can mark up some local gains. Several times during this century Britain has magnanimously come to terms with a formerly subject people—as with South Africa after the Boer War, and with the countries of our former Indian Empire. On other occasions, for example in Ireland after the rebellion, in Cyprus, in many of the former colonies, we have learned to yield more or less gracefully.

Within our own society we are still deeply divided by differences of class, and yet these differences have been considerably reduced since 1900. Attitudes of subservience towards members of the upper classes are now less frequently shown, or expected. Each world war was followed by a stride forward towards greater social equality, stimulated, I believe, by the sense of solidarity we experienced as a nation through sharing hardships and dangers in common. We look back now with pride to 1940 when we as a nation stood alone against apparently overwhelming odds; but in the perspective of history perhaps equal importance will be given to the years immediately after the war. This was the time when our people attained a new level of responsible concern for their fellow-citizens, a concern which found expression in the provisions of the Welfare State.

This climate of opinion also made it possible for us to take the lead in community planning, in which architecture is informed by the findings of sociological research in the design of urban environments which will be both attractive and functional.[2] In our social legislation during this century, we have shown that we still have a particular aptitude for evolving institutions such as the Medical Research Council and the B.B.C., which show a compromise between complete autonomy and governmental control: a compromise which may not be logical, but which seems to work.

I would like now to consider what changes may come about in British life during the rest of this century. I propose to consider our future first from the standpoint of the biologist, and then from that of the social historian, before venturing to speculate about the influences these changes may have upon our national character.

Biologists are accustomed to thinking in very long time-perspectives. The physical evolution of our species has been slow and very prolonged; but during the centuries of recorded history something new, and unique to man, has entered the picture. This is man's ability to transmit ideas from one generation to the next, and to add to these ideas. All of our

leading biologists, men like J. Z. Young, Medawar, Waddington and Huxley, have emphasized this new element in human
development; they insist that social and psychological innova-
tions now predominate over the much slower processes of
biological change, in the continuing evolution of mankind.[3]

These new concepts in evolutionary theory have been advanced with great imaginative force by the late Teilhard de
Chardin, who viewed all the millennia of biological development as merely preparing the way for man's spiritual and
intellectual evolution, which has scarcely begun.[4] He has
compared the mounting acceleration of human thought to
the thrust of a rocket when its second-stage motor begins to
fire. Teilhard has been taken to task for using language and
concepts which belong more to poetry than to science,[5] but his
merit is that he conveys the excitement and the scope of the
new possibilities before mankind.

All this, however, belongs to the realm of speculation; and
this speculation is darkened by the constant reminder that man
has discovered, and perfected, the means of his own destruction
—and may yet employ them.

Although biologists agree about the enormously increased
rate of human psycho-social evolution, they tend still to think
in terms of generations, if not of centuries or millennia. When
we lower our horizon to the limits of the present century we
can more confidently predict the outcome of certain dominant
trends in recent social and political history.

Until quite recent times, every major culture had its own
traditions, its own cosmology, its own interpretation of the
nature and significance of man (which was usually formulated
in terms of man's relationship to God). But during the last
hundred years, and with increasing momentum during the last
few decades, something quite new has supervened. We have
seen the growing acceptance, in *every* culture, of a similar *eidos*,
or way of thinking, based upon the scientific method.

It is difficult for a non-scientist to realize the full force of the torrent of scientific discovery. Professor Oppenheimer recently expressed this vividly. He said that the pursuit of scientific knowledge as a whole-time occupation is so new a phenomenon that 93 per cent. of all full-time scientists who ever lived are still alive today. He went on to illustrate the enormous increase of information in every special field of inquiry.[6]

This explosive expansion of scientific knowledge, crossing all national frontiers, and its application to agricultural and industrial production and especially to communications, introduce something quite new into human experience. They are creating a mental climate favourable to new forms of political organizations, world-wide in their scope.

It is no longer utopian to envisage a single world government administering the affairs of mankind: our own future history as a nation must be seen in relation to developments on these lines.

The greatest obstacle is no longer a material one: the technical resources are already available to make this possible. The obstacle now lies in men's minds: it lies in the fact that we are still obsessed by age-old fears and enmities.

I do not underestimate this difficulty. We are all well aware of our conscious fear, fear of what the other side will do with their weapons of annihilation. There are genuine conflicts of interest between nations, which give rise to quite rational anxieties. But in addition to this, we are very prone to ascribe evil intentions to each other; and I believe that we do this because we have not come to terms with the evil within ourselves.

Here is a territory in which religion and psychiatry meet. Religion talks in terms of guilt, and of the way in which the seven deadly sins obscure our vision of God's purpose for mankind. Psychiatry also deals with guilt and with the conflicts in our own personalities which prevent our seeing things clearly. Both the religious and the psychiatric interpretations of our present predicament suggest that we shall only be freed from fear of each other when we recognize, and abate, our own destructive impulses. An involuntary bias of this kind often has its origin in experiences of childhood.

In an earlier talk I deplored the emotional impoverishment of the family groups in which many children in our community spend their formative years. These children grow up with personalities crippled by the economics of scarcity: scarcity above all of affection and emotional security, which renders them liable, in later life, to personal isolation, suspicion and despair. It may be instructive to compare this situation with that of thirty, or fifty or a hundred years ago, when a much higher proportion of children grew up in homes which were not only emotionally but also materially impoverished. We have made progress in reducing the amount of severe poverty in our society: our next task is to try to ensure that children are not deprived of the emotional sustenance which they need in order to develop into well-balanced beings.

It is a commonplace that large groups of people tend to react in an even more emotional, less rational way than individuals. As individuals we have been learning how to recognize the limits of our rationality, and how to extend these limits. As nations, we shall have to learn to do the same. The first step in this direction is to realize that there are some aspects of our own thinking and behaviour which other people can judge more clearly than we ourselves are able to do; the next and greater step is to accept other people's judgments about our behaviour.

I believe that Britain is well placed to give a lead to other countries in this process of self-abnegation because we have succeeded in accepting the loss of a great deal of our former power and influence without losing our self-respect.

Misfortune, when it is not overwhelming, can make a

person more self-critical, more insightful, less egocentric. Perhaps something of this kind has been altering our own national consciousness during the last generation, in which we have seen the progressive dismantling of the British Empire. We are gradually learning to stop thinking of ourselves as one of the Great Powers.

The concentration of military power in the hands of the U.S.S.R. and the U.S.A. has completely changed our role, as the Cuba crisis clearly demonstrated. For some days we became acutely aware of ourselves as an island armed like Cuba with the rockets and hydrogen bombs of a much stronger allied power and subject to swift annihilation if war should break out.

In our own social history, we may expect the continuation of our halting progress towards a more equalitarian society. If the methods of scientific experiment and validation become increasingly adopted by social scientists—as I believe they will —future experiments in social reform will tend to be designed on experimental lines, so that whether they succeed or not, they will add to our knowledge. Neither science nor sociology, however, can provide the values which ultimately inspire such interventions. I suggest that the ultimate value behind attempts to remedy the diverse patterns of social failure is simply this: a belief in the individual worth, and dignity, of every human being. This is a value to which both humanists and Christians subscribe.

As I see it, the new problems which we shall have to face during the next few years will not be unique to Britain, although the way we tackle them may be influenced by our particular history and resources. We can expect, for example, some new emphases in education. During the rest of this century the mountainous accumulation of scientific information is likely to continue. Pupils of the future cannot possible digest all the facts. Fortunately, this is a task which we shall soon be able to delegate to computors and electronic storehouses of factual data. Machines will relieve us of the drudgery of calculation and free us to devote more time to other studies: to learning the principles on which scientific hypotheses are based; to cultivating an appreciation of literature and the arts; and to developing a clearer understanding of our own personalities and our deeper motivations.

This will not be achieved simply by letting the teaching of psychology and human personality development take its proper place beside biology in school and university curricula. Insight into the workings of one's own mind can best be acquired through experience in groups, or in an individual relationship discussed personally with one's teacher. This type of learning, which is similar to that of a disciple and his *guru,* or an apprentice and his master, already forms part of the training of every would-be psychotherapist. It cultivates a self-awareness which will, I believe, become part of the intellectual equipment of every well-educated man and woman.

But I do not regard this cultivation of greater insight as the prerogative only of the university graduates of the future. I believe that its influence will spread throughout society, through newspapers, broadcasting and whatever new mass media the future may discover. One has only to study the quite abstruse conventions implicit in modern films, and in radio or television plays, to realize the considerable advance in sophistication shown by popular audiences during the last forty years.

The new psychological sophistication, if it can be achieved, would be shown not by the use of neo-Freudian jargon, but by the recognition in everyday speech and behaviour, of clues to people's unconscious as well as to their conscious motivation.

It may seem incongruous to think of ourselves as a people becoming more psychologically perceptive. This seems at variance with our traditions, in which sensitivity has generally been subordinated to the predominance of rather philistine practical men and women; and yet there has always been a strong element of poetry and imagination in our country.

A by-product of this process of self-understanding is that it tends to make one less censorious of other people's peculiarities, including those of our own teenagers. Eccentricity is a social asset in a world full of stereotypes. Perhaps there will be fewer misfits in our society if we learn to emulate the Indians in their remarkable tolerance for harmless eccentrics.

I have repeatedly referred to material, intellectual and social changes which appear to have outstripped our imaginative grasp.

Perhaps the outstanding example of this today is the hydrogen bomb. We know, intellectually, that these bombs have introduced a quite new factor into international politics; and yet many people do not seem to have grasped its full implications. Of course in this, as in other matters, there are some people who recognize the significance of the new phenomenon before the rest of us, some who think ahead. But whereas in former times we were usually given at least a generation in which to get used to each new discovery, now major changes invade and transform social life several times in each generation.[7] We shall have to get used to this.

Because of the constant growth of knowledge, it is truer now than ever before that education is a lifelong process. This may have practical consequences; to take one example, today a doctor must pass strict examinations in order to be allowed to practise; but his knowledge will be out of date within ten years. Already many doctors are taking advantage of regular refresher courses in order to keep in touch with new developments. So far, these courses are optional, and as a result those who most need them are least likely to attend; perhaps before long every doctor should be required to study again, and to pass exams again, at intervals of five or ten years.

Nor will the Church be immune from this pressure for change. Far-sighted leaders of every denomination have already seen that they must repeatedly re-examine their teachings in the light of contemporary knowledge and events if they are to continue to play a part in influencing men's minds.

I referred earlier in this talk to the rapid growth throughout the world of scientific thinking and of its practical applications. This triumph of technology carries with it the danger of imposing a uniformity of material objects and of ideas. Paradoxically, this very threat may prove a godsend to the creative arts. During the present century many of our poets and painters have felt alienated from a society which seemed to deny them any essential role: but now they have a definite role again.

Today, many commodities have become steroetyped and internationally interchangeable, and this has even affected the arts. Action painting and abstract impressionism have been produced with depressing uniformity in every part of the world, but this universality has been accompanied by a sacrifice of emotional significance. An artist's work expresses feelings which are at once intensely personal, and communicable to others: but this communication is most effective when his experiences are linked with a particular place and time.

I suggest that the creative artist's role in the future may be to keep alive the sense of significance in local and national traditions, and so to combat the deadening effect of uniformity. This, I believe, is the justification of even such small sub-cultural groups as the Lallans poets, who write poetry with a Scots accent.

I must confess that much of Lallans is Greek to me, and yet sometimes I catch the excitement of feelings which can only be expressed in one's mother tongue; for example, when Hugh MacDiarmid likens the moonlit earth to the tear-streaked face of a sleeping child in his line:

'Earth, thou bonnie broukit bairn'[8]

Or again, in Sidney Goodsir Smith's verse:

'Oh weary fa' the day maun daw
Oh weary fa' the sun
Oh weary fa' the bonnie bird
That tells the nicht is run.'[9]

I admire Lallans verse, not only for the snatches of lyric poetry which are immediately intelligible, but as one facet of our many-sided island culture. It is a reminder that we shall participate most fruitfully in the coming world community if we keep alive a good measure of our eccentricities, our private visions and our peculiar variations on the pattern of mankind.

NOTES

1 For this quotation I am indebted to Sir Geoffrey Vickers, V.C., who cited it in his Wilde Memorial Lecture 'Some Ideas of Progress', *Memoirs and Proceedings of the Manchester Literary and Philosophical Society*, **96**, 2, 1 (1954-55).

2 Descriptions of post-war community planning in Britain can be found in (*a*) Report of the *Ministry of Housing and Local Government, 1960*. Cmnd. 1435, London. H.M.S.O., 1961. (*b*) Nicholson, J. H. *New Communities in Britain*. London: National Council for Social Service, 1961. (*c*) Jennings, Hilda: *Societies in the Making*. London: Routledge & Kegan Paul, 1962.

3 Young, J. Z. *Doubt and Certainty in Science, The Reith Lectures for 1950*. London: Oxford Univ. Press, 1951.
Medawar, P. B. *The Future of Man*. London: Methuen, 1960.
Waddington, C. H. *The Nature of Life*. London: Allen & Unwin, 1960.
Huxley, J. S. *The Humanist Frame*. London: Allen & Unwin, 1961. New York: Harper, 1961.
Huxley, J. S. 'Higher and Lower Organization in Evolution', *J. R. Coll. Surg. Edin.* **7**, 163, 1962.

4 Teilhard de Chardin. *The Phenomenon of Man*. Trans. B. Wall. London: Collins, 1959.

5 Medawar, P. B. 'Critical Notice: P. Teilhard de Chardin, *The Phenomenon of Man*', *Mind*, **70**, 99, 1961.

6 Oppenheimer, R. J. 'Science and Culture', *Encounter*, October 1962.

7 A listener wrote to draw my attention to A. N. Whitehead's words: 'In the past the time-span of important changes was considerably longer than that of a single human life. Thus mankind was trained to adapt itself to fixed conditions. Today this time-span is considerably shorter than that of human life, and accordingly our training must prepare individuals to face a novelty of conditions.' *Adventures of Ideas*, Cambridge Univ. Press, 1933. London: Penguin Books, 1948.

8 Grieve, C. M. (Hugh MacDiarmid). This poem was published in his volume *Sangschaw*. Edinburgh: Blackwood, 1925. It has been reproduced in several anthologies, including John Buchan's *The Northern Muse* and J. Oliver and J. C. Smith's *A Scots Anthology*.

9 Smith, S. Goodsir. Saltire Modern Poets Series. Edinburgh: Oliver & Boyd, 1947.